The
Complete Muffin
C·O·O·K·B·O·O·K

THE ULTIMATE GUIDE TO MAKING GREAT MUFFINS

Gloria Ambrosia

SQUAREONE
PUBLISHERS

COVER DESIGNER: Jacqueline Michelus and Jeannie Tudor
COVER PHOTO: Getty Images, Inc.
INTERIOR ART: John Wincek
EDITOR: Marie Caratozzolo
TYPESETTER: Gary A. Rosenberg

Square One Publishers
115 Herricks Road
Garden City Park, NY 11040
(516) 535-2010 • (877) 900-BOOK
www.squareonepublishers.com

Library of Congress Cataloging-in-Publication Data

Ambrosia, Gloria.
    The complete muffin cookbook : the ultimate guide to making
great muffins / Gloria Ambrosia.
        p. cm.
    Includes index.
    ISBN 0-7570-0179-3
    1. Muffins. I. Title.
    TX770.M83A48   2006
    641.8'157—dc22

                                                          2005021727

Printed in the United States of America

10   9   8   7   6   5   4   3   2   1

Contents

Preface

When I told my family and friends I planned to write a muffin cookbook, the first question they asked was, "What are you going to do with all the test muffins?" As you can imagine, there was no shortage of people willing to sample and critique my lastest creations. That was fine with me because, while there are many reasons I love to cook, I most enjoy seeing smiling faces and hearing the "Mmms" of the people who eat delicious food prepared with a loving heart. Muffins have a way of calling forth the loudest "Mmms" of all. Muffins make us happy, and when we are happy, life is a little easier.

Delighting people with muffins has become a bit of a religion with me. I imagine that my mission is to lighten people's hearts—and even turn scowls to smiles and grumbles to grins—with muffins. One of my idols is a Buddhist holy woman whose delicious cooking made a group of monks so happy that they were able to break through a stalemate in their meditation and attain the fullest fruits of their spiritual quest.

Matika-mata lived on the edge of a forest where thirty monks practiced meditation and strove toward enlightenment. Like many devout Buddhists, she would get up before dawn each day in order to prepare food for the monks' daily alms round. One day, Matika-mata asked to visit the monastery to receive instruction in meditation. She did as the monks had instructed and within a short period of time realized full enlightenment. It is said that her concentration was so deep that she also attained great mental powers, including the ability to read minds.

Having attained such high wisdom, she realized that none of the monks at the monastery had developed their meditation practice to the same extent. Puzzled, she used her powers of mind to probe into the mind of each monk to ascertain the reason why. To her amazement, she discovered that the monks were unhappy because they were not getting the foods they liked to eat! This unhappiness dominated their states of mind and made it difficult for them to practice meditation with delight—a necessary ingredient for one who wishes to realize liberation.

Matika-mata used her powers of mind to discover each monk's favorite food. From that day forward she would arise well before dawn and prepare exactly what each monk liked to eat—thirty different dishes! The monks were very happy (although they were not allowed to show it), and their happy states of mind lasted throughout the day. Before long, each monk attained the full fruits of meditation practice! Matika-mata's reputation grew, for it was said that the meals she prepared lead to enlightenment. Monks came from far and wide to practice in the forest near where she lived.

While I can't guarantee that my muffins will lead to enlightenment, they will most certainly make everyone who eats them very happy. My idea in writing this book was to challenge muffins to the limits of their potential by creating interesting, nutritious, and delicious muffins made from reasonably priced and easy-to-find ingredients.

That's how this cookbook came about. First, I gathered together my favorite recipes, making no distinction between cakes, breads, casseroles, soups, or desserts. I even considered my favorite candy and ice cream. Then I created a muffin to capture the flavors in each. I discovered that muffins can be made out of anything. And I mean anything! And it can be done without compromising nutrition or cost. This cookbook proves it.

What this cookbook *disproves* is the common conception that muffins are just for breakfast. I ask you, "Why stop there?" With the right combination of ingredients, muffins make a great dessert or after-school snack. You can take muffins along on camping trips and picnics, too. Leave out the sweetener and add veggies, herbs, or cheese, and you've got great savory muffins to accompany soups, salads, or a full-course meal. And what could be more versatile for special occasions and parties than muffins? With these ideas in mind I developed six chapters filled with scrumptuous muffins for every occassion—or for no occasion at all!

Like Matika-mata, you will find, I am sure, many recipes to delight and uplift the hearts of your loved ones. And don't be surprised if friends and relations start coming from far and wide to be near you and to enjoy the fruits of your labor.

Introduction

There is no love sincerer than the love of food.

—GEORGE BERNARD SHAW

Muffins are on the rise, if you will pardon my pun. I mean, folks have been turning in their direction. Sure, muffins have long been a favorite treat, but never more so than in recent years. With all the talk about saturated fats, high blood cholesterol, and the need for more fiber and less sugar in our diets, muffins make sense. You can use oils that are low in saturated fats, whole grains that are high in fiber, and natural unrefined sweeteners. And muffins are quick and easy to make.

I turned to muffins for all these reasons and more. You see, I have quite a history with baked goods—especially breads and sweet cakes like coffeecake and donuts. You might say we have a personal relationship. When I was a kid, I used to eat six or eight slices of raisin toast for breakfast. Mmm, mmm. My mom couldn't understand where I was putting it! Then for lunch, I'd take a couple of peanut butter sandwiches with a cream-filled cupcake or two for dessert—every day. When I learned in history class that the Romans conquered the world by feeding their soldiers grains and breads three times a day, I could really relate to what the soldiers had experienced. I figured that the soldiers must have been very happy people. You know what I mean? They must have *felt* as though they could conquer the world.

Over the years, I have tempered my youthful passions for gooey sweet breads and cakes made with refined ingredients. For one thing, I notice that I feel better when I have more whole grain fiber in my diet. The bulk does my system good. I also notice that sugar highs hurt more than delight me. The overall sluggishness I experience on the heels of consuming a glazed donut is too high a price for the few moments of pleasure while eating it. Research on cholesterol consumption and its correlation with heart disease has made me take a closer look at my tendency to put gobs of butter on bread or an inch of icing on a cake made with five eggs and a cup and a half of butter.

But my sweet tooth is still with me. All my teeth are sweet! So in recent years, I've searched for baked goods that satisfy my pining for sweets without compromising my desire for good nutrition. Is it any wonder I've turned to the natural sweetness of muffins? Sometimes it's the most ordinary things in life that bring about the most extraordinary delights, isn't it? When it comes down to it, I'd rather bake muffins than any other kind of baked good. Muffins are quick and easy to bake. Even if the need arises suddenly, I can have a batch ready in twenty minutes.

Muffins are about as perfect as food gets. I mean, how often do you find a basic food item that is not only wholesome and nutritious but also delicious, heart-healthy, immensely satisfying, and suitable for enjoying any time of day? And *baking* muffins is one of the most pleasurable experiences in the world—not to mention one of the nicest things we can do for ourselves and the people we love. Making muffins with all these attractive qualities is simply a matter of gathering together the proper ingredients, and then preparing and combining them in such a way as to ensure success. Of course, you also need fabulous recipes—which is why I wrote this book!

1. Helpful **Hints** and **Information**

In the beginner's mind there are many possibilities.
—ZEN MASTER SUZUKI ROSHI

During my years of muffin making, I have experimented with different ingredients, equipment, and procedures. Muffins are easy to make, it's true. But experience separates the mediocre muffin makers from the fabulous ones. I've prepared this section to help you benefit from my experience. Trust me. I've worked out the kinks and can help you make better muffins. This chapter is intended to take the guesswork out of muffin making and help you become a fabulous muffin baker.

INGREDIENTS

I've taken measures to create muffin recipes from wholesome and nutritious ingredients that are readily available at your local grocery and health food stores. These days, one-stop shopping is possible in most cities and towns because more and more grocery chains are carrying products that were once available only at health food and specialty food stores. When you shop, you should have no trouble finding the ingredients you need to bake.

I like to keep a basic supply of muffin ingredients on hand at all times. This is not difficult because most of the ingredients store easily and for long periods of time. I have designated a cupboard and a special corner in my refrigerator just for muffin ingredients, and I try to keep these areas well stocked. Then, whenever the urge hits me, I can bake just about any muffin in my repertoire. What follows is my suggested list of muffin-making staples. You'll notice that all of the dairy products on the list are for regular muffins, not low-fat. Of course, if you tend to be more of a low-fat muffin maker, keep low-fat or fat-free dairy products on hand.

❏ Baking powder.

❏ Baking soda.

❏ Bran: oat and wheat.

❏ Chocolate: mini semi-sweet chocolate chips.

❏ Cocoa powder.

❏ Coconut, flaked.

❏ Cornmeal: blue, white, and/or yellow.

❏ Dairy products: buttermilk, milk, sour cream, cream cheese.

❏ Dried fruits: apricots, currants, prunes, raisins, mixed dried fruit bits.

❏ Eggs.

❏ Extracts: almond, rum, vanilla, and any other flavors you like and use.

❏ Flours: brown rice, buckwheat, oat, rye, soy, unbleached white, whole wheat, whole wheat pastry.

❏ Granola, homemade or store bought.

❏ Lemon and orange peel.

❏ Nuts: almonds, pecans, walnuts.

❏ Oats, rolled.

❏ Salt.

❏ Shortening: butter, canola oil, margarine, olive oil.

❏ Sweeteners: apple juice concentrates, applesauce, light and dark brown sugars, fresh fruit, honey, maple syrup, molasses.

❏ Wheat germ, toasted.

What follows next is a closer look at these ingredients, which I consider muffin-making basics.

FLOUR

This is going to sound crazy, but when I eat whole grains, I feel like I am eating the earth itself. Don't get me wrong. It's not that whole grains taste like dirt. It's that eating them makes me feel elementally connected with the substance of life—earth, air, heat, and water. Grains, and especially baked goods that are made with them, are the body's ambrosia. I think that is why we feel so good inside when we eat whole grains.

For the majority of my muffin recipes, I have called for whole wheat, whole wheat pastry, and unbleached white flours because they are the varieties most readily available—and I wanted to make it easy for you to enjoy the goodness of nutritious muffins. My selection of flour depends upon the flavor, texture, and density I seek. There is no magical formula, just preference.

Up to now, you may have believed that muffins made with unrefined flours are squat, dense, and unappealing. I'm here to tell you they don't have to be. Many factors (ingredients, preparation procedures, and oven temperature) combine to determine muffin lightness. Your choice of flours is only one of them. Nutritious muffins baked with rich whole-grain flours need not have the consistency of freeze-dried lead. If you take the time to sift, you can use any type of flour you want and still bake a relatively light muffin. You will also need to pay attention to rising agents, egg preparation, oven temperature, and the amount of stirring. All these factors are explained in the following pages.

If you think the only way to produce a well-shaped muffin is by using unbleached white flour, suit yourself. You can substitute up to a half cup of unbleached white flour for the required flours in any given recipe. But if you are willing to stretch your efforts and try muffins that incorporate a greater variety of whole-grain flours, I know you will be pleasantly surprised. I use a broad range of flours in my muffin recipes. As I just mentioned, most call for whole wheat, whole wheat pastry, and unbleached white flours, but I am also fond of barley, brown rice, buckwheat, rye, and soy flours, as well as cornmeal and rolled oats. These add variety to muffins in both flavor and nutrition. For the nutritional analysis of these flours, see Table 1.1 on pages 6 and 7.

TABLE 1.1 NUTRIENT ANALYSIS IN FLOURS, CORNMEALS, AND OATS				
Product (1-cup serving)	Total calories	Fat grams	Cholesterol mgs	Protein grams
Barley Flour	400	2	0	14
Brown Rice Flour	600	3	0	12
Buckwheat Flour	400	4	0	16
Cornmeal, Yellow	434	4	0	10
Cornmeal, White	434	4	0	10
Oats, Rolled	300	6	0	10
Rye Flour	400	2	0	12
Soy Flour	400	18	0	32
White Flour (unbleached)	400	1	0	12
Whole Wheat Flour	400	2	0	15
Whole Wheat Pastry Flour	303	2	0	10

Whole Wheat Flour

When I eat cooked wheat berries I get some insight into why wheat, in its many forms, is consumed in larger quantities worldwide than any other cereal grain. The cooked berry is hearty, chewy, and satisfying to the taste. I can actually feel the wholesome goodness going to work on my body, making it strong and healthy.

Whole wheat is high in protein, fiber, and complex carbohydrates. It also contains vitamin E and several important B vitamins. But in order to get the full measure of benefits from wheat, one would have to eat the entire wheat berry—including the bran (the outer layer, which constitutes about 14 percent of the wheat kernel's total weight), the wheat germ (the embryo or seed, which makes up about 3 percent of the weight), and the endosperms (the starchy middle part, which comprises 83 percent of the weight).

Fiber grams	Carbs grams	Sodium mgs	Calcium mgs	Iron mgs	Potassium mgs
19.4	86	4	20	1.8	182
3.0	132	15	60	3.2	393
12.0	84	0	0	4.3	700
8.8	92	42	7	4.2	344
8.8	92	42	7	4.2	344
8.0	54	0	0	3.6	280
9.7	83	0	20	4.5	230
16.0	32	0	160	9.0	1500
3.4	86	0	0	4.5	140
13.0	80	10	20	3.6	420
9.1	67	0	61	3.3	348

Whole wheat flour is just that—the whole wheat berry that has been milled into a fine powder. All of the nutritional components of the whole wheat kernel are intact. Highly processed flour, on the other hand, contains only the endosperms, the part with the least nutritional value. When buying whole wheat flour, make certain the package says it is 100-percent whole wheat. This means the flour has been made from the whole wheat berry and nothing has been processed out.

Whole Wheat Pastry Flour

Whole wheat pastry flour is made from soft red winter wheat, not the hard variety that is used to make whole wheat flour. It is still considered whole wheat flour in that it has been milled from the whole wheat berry, but whole wheat pastry flour is lighter. A cup of whole wheat flour weighs 113 grams, while a cup of whole wheat pastry flour weighs only 90 grams. Whole wheat pastry flour also has less protein than hard winter wheat flour—10 grams as compared to 15 grams.

One might think that the lightness of whole wheat pastry flour would make it a more desirable choice for muffins than regular whole wheat flour. But the lightness of the flour doesn't necessarily mean that the muffins will rise more. In fact, it is the presence of protein in wheat that makes the batter rise during baking; and whole wheat pastry flour contains less protein than regular whole wheat. I've noticed that if I use only whole wheat pastry flour in a muffin recipe, the muffins are not as successful as when I also add whole wheat flour.

Whole wheat pastry flour does not absorb moisture in the same way as other flours. So, it is only interchangeable with other flours up to $\frac{1}{4}$ to $\frac{1}{3}$ cup. Beyond that amount, you'll need to reduce the amount of liquid. You can substitute whole wheat pastry flour with equal amounts of regular whole wheat and unbleached white flour in any of my recipes.

Unbleached White Flour

I used to shy away from using too much unbleached white flour, thinking it less desirable than whole wheat. I've warmed up to it. While it's true that unbleached white flour contains less fiber than its less-refined parent product, it also contains less fat. Besides, you can easily compensate for the comparatively weaker nutritional makeup of unbleached white flour by using it in combination with whole wheat flour or by adding wheat or oat bran to balance things out.

You may be interested to know that there are brands of unbleached white flour available at your local health food store that retain some of the bran and germ. These are usually called "whole grain white flours."

Barley Flour

I have a theory that if we paid closer attention to the flavor of the foods we eat, we would quite naturally eat what is good for us. Barley is a good example. This grain is so delicious and so satisfying that sometimes I cook up a big bowl of whole grain barley and eat it all by itself. Mmm. And I find I don't want to add anything to it—except maybe a dash of soy sauce.

As seen in Table 1.1 on pages 6 and 7, barley flour has lots of cholesterol-lowering fiber —more than six times the fiber in brown rice and unbleached white flours and twice the amount in rye and whole wheat pastry flours. Besides, barley is more easily digested than wheat, which is why it is so often used in baby food. When our digestion is good, we tend to be bright and alert. The trouble is, in order to enjoy the cholesterol-reducing properties from the grain, we need to eat it in its whole grain form, and most of the commercially available barley and barley flour has been processed to remove the outer hull. *Pearling*, as the process is called, destroys almost all the fiber and about half the nutrients.

Many health food stores sell flour made from hulled barley (barley that retains its hull). If this more nutritious variety isn't available, maybe they will be willing to order it for you.

Brown Rice Flour

Like barley flour, brown rice flour is made from hulled whole grain rice (rice that has not been processed to remove the outer hull). And like barley flour, brown rice flour is sweet to the taste, making it an ideal ingredient for muffins. It derives its sweetness from an abundance of complex carbohydrates—132 grams per cup of flour compared to only 80 grams in whole wheat flour and 67 in whole wheat pastry flour. Complex carbohydrates, with their slow, steady digestibility, are the best source of energy for our bodies. Muffins that are made with brown rice flour are like the Eveready Energizer battery. They help us keep going and going and going.

Buckwheat Flour

I have found that there are two kinds of people in the world—those who like buckwheat and those who don't. I'm one of the former. I like the way its strong, nutty flavor dominates a muffin and gives it that special taste. It is particularly delicious when combined with maple syrup. In addition to its distinctive flavor, buckwheat is high in protein and fiber. It is also very high in potassium, a nutrient necessary to regulate and maintain proper fluid balance and blood pressure, and very low in fat, containing only 1 gram of fat in each two-ounce serving.

Buckwheat flour comes in two varieties: light and dark. Light buckwheat flour is usually made from the whole seed minus the hard outer shell, while the darker variety contains both the seed and most of its hull. Dark buckwheat flour is the more nutritious of the two. In fact, it contains more protein per measure than any other kind of "grain." (Actually, buckwheat is not wheat at all. In fact, it is not even a grain; it is the seed of an herb!) If the flour has dark flecks that look something like the vanilla bean flecks in better ice creams, you'll know it is dark buckwheat flour. Buy it. It'll knock your socks off.

Rolled Oats, Oat Flour, and Oat Bran

There are many reasons for using rolled oats, oat flour, and oat bran in muffins. For starters, they have a sweet and pleasing flavor. (What can I say? I always seem to weigh that factor first.) They also contain a natural antioxidant that helps keep muffins moist, reducing the need for fat or oil. A good source of carbohydrates, protein, B vitamins and minerals, oats are also considered one of the most nutritionally complete of all grains. But perhaps most important, a considerable amount of scientific research has linked the consumption of oats, particularly oat bran, with low cholesterol levels. It is believed that cholesterol sticks to the soluble fiber in oat bran and is thereby flushed out of the body easily.

What distinguishes rolled oats from oat flour and oat bran? Oats are commonly pre- pared by flattening the whole grain or *groat* into a disk. *Rolling,* as the process is called, makes the oats easier to cook, but does not rob the grain of its nutritional value.

Oats can also be milled into flour for use in baking. During the milling process, the bran can be removed from the oats and packaged separately. Look for oat bran among the hot cereals in your grocery store.

Cornmeal

What I said about barley can also be said about cornmeal. It's the good tasting things in life that are often the best for us. Cornmeal is an excellent source of fiber and complex carbohydrates. Its sweet, nutty flavor makes it a popular ingredient for muffins.

Always purchase cornmeal that has been stone-ground or water-ground. Unlike other milling processes for corn, these grinding techniques do not remove the hull and germ—the most nutritious parts of the corn kernel. And milling corn in this way diminishes the likelihood that muffins made with cornmeal will crumble all to bits when you slice or bite into them. (You know, the way some cornmeal muffins do!)

Rye Flour

Rye flour, which is quite popular, is found next to the whole wheat flours and cornmeals in most grocery stores. Surprisingly high in fiber, rye flour contains more than three times the amount found in brown rice flour and unbleached white flour. Most commercial brands of rye flour are primarily wheat, so read the label before buying. Be sure the product contains only rye flour or that the rye is listed first among the ingredients.

Dark rye flour is made from whole rye berries and has the nutrition of whole grain rye intact. The package usually reads "whole grain" rye flour. Light and medium rye flours, however, have had the bran and/or germ removed, which means much of the nutritional value is gone.

Soy Flour

The appeal of soy flour is its nutritional value. While it contains much more fat per measure than any other flour (18 grams per cup compared to 2 grams in whole wheat flour), it also contains more than twice the protein of most other flours and nearly twice the fiber.

I suppose I'd use soy flour more liberally if it weren't for the fact that it's pungent and bitter tasting, and surprisingly heavy. If you add too much to muffins, they come out dense and flat. Not at all desirable. So I use soy flour only in those muffins that I feel could use a little protein boost, and I use only two to four tablespoons per batch. Some soy flours have been treated or slightly toasted to improve flavor and digestibility. When buying soy flour, ask for these types.

RISING AGENTS

Did you ever notice that some muffins rise more than others? Me, too. In my early days of muffin making, I drove myself crazy trying to make all my muffins the same size and shape. I finally realized that it's impossible. Muffins are like people. They come in all shapes and sizes. Different combinations of ingredients produce different-shaped muffins. That's all there is to it.

Muffins that are made with heavier, denser ingredients, such as whole wheat flour, dried fruits, or fruit purées, are going to be slightly heavier and denser than those made with lighter flours. Likewise, muffins that are made with ingredients such as sour cream or yogurt always seems to sit taller in the saddle. That's part of what makes muffins so interesting.

Having said that, I must add that you can optimize the rising action of your muffins by selecting the right rising agent for the job. The idea is to produce batter that is not so acidic that it bubbles out of control before you have a chance to put it in the oven, and yet not so alkaline that it has no oomph at all.

Baking powder is a nicely balanced combination of acid powder (cream of tartar) and alkaline powder (bicarbonate of soda). It produces batter with the right kind of rising action. Because many of my batters contain such acidic ingredients as fruit purées, citrus peel, and honey, I balance the rising action by using baking soda in combination with baking powder.

When buying rising agents, bear in mind that they do not have a long shelf life. If your muffins are consistently turning out flat and squat, it's probably because your rising agent is flat and squat. Throw it out and buy a fresh supply. If you bake infrequently, buy small packages.

If you ever run out of baking powder, don't worry. Mix cream of tartar and bicarbonate of soda, two-to-one, and measure the mixture as you would commerial baking powder. It's essentially the same thing.

SALT

Salt enhances the flavors in muffins. The trick is to select a pure salt product and not use too much of it.

What we commonly know as table salt is pure sodium chloride with added iodine. Because it is mined from inland deposits that are millions of years old, all the useful trace minerals have long since evaporated. In addition, regular table salt usually contains additives designed to make it more free-flowing. A better choice than regular table salt might be a low-sodium salt product that contains 33 percent less sodium and is iodine-free. However, I believe an even better choice is sea salt. High in trace minerals, sea salt is obtained from evaporated sea water. It contains no sugar or chemical additives.

Table salt. Low-sodium salt. Sea salt. Use whichever makes sense to you. When I use salt in my muffins, it is in very small amounts— usually only $\frac{1}{4}$ teaspoon per batch.

SWEETENERS

I have never liked overly sweet muffins. There's a restaurant in my town that serves a walnut muffin that is so sweet I can taste the sugar on my lips long after I've taken a bite. Yuk! It's really not a muffin at all. It's a cupcake. I want the sweetness of my muffins to be more subtle than that.

To achieve the subtle sweet taste I like, I rely on the wholesome goodness of fresh fruit, fruit juice concentrates, dried fruit, and fruit purées; the syrupy sweetness of honey, molasses, and maple syrup; the robust flavor of brown sugar; and occasionally, when I am trying to achieve a more dessert-like muffin, table sugar. I also use what I call my magic ingredients—spices, extracts, and citrus peel. These perk up the natural flavors of muffins and give the illusion of added sweetness.

Fruit

Many of my recipes call for fruit—apples, ripe bananas, blueberries, dark sweet cherries, mangoes, peaches, pears, and raspberries. I like using fruit because, in addition to being high in complex carbohydrates (the energy nutrient), it is also high in fiber. And fruit is convenient to use. Fresh apples and bananas are available year round, while most other fruits are always available frozen or canned.

Fruit Purée

In the process of creating muffins for this cookbook, I discovered the value of common fruit purées, such as apple butter and applesauce. I also make fruit purées from a variety of fresh and canned fruit—peaches, apricots, and mangos. These not only sweeten the pot, they also moisten the batter, diminishing the need for fat or oil. According to a manufacturer of prune and apple butters, substituting purées for the shortening in baked goods reduces the fat content by 75 to 90 percent and the calories by 20 to 30 percent.

Fruit Juice and Fruit Juice Concentrates

Fruit juice and fruit juice concentrates give muffins a natural sweetness. However, I have learned to limit the use of these ingredients because too much can cause the muffins to burn, often before they are fully cooked. I never use more than a half cup of fruit juice or fruit juice concentrate per batch of muffins.

When buying these items, check the ingredients to make sure they do not contain added sugar. The natural products are sweet enough.

Dried Fruit

Dried fruits are great muffin sweeteners. They are particularly handy because, when properly stored, they have a long shelf life. Apples, apricots, dates, figs, grapes, peaches, pears, and plums are the most popular dried fruits. While these varieties are readily available in most grocery and health food stores, you may have to search the specialty shops for the dried cranberries and raspberries that I use in some of my muffins. Trust me. It will be worth the effort.

For many years, it seemed that one fruit-preserving company dominated the market. Recently, however, perhaps because of our increased interest in dried fruit as a low-fat snack, I have seen and sampled quality products from lesser-known companies. This is good for consumers, as it helps ensure competitive prices.

Honey

Although chemically, honey is not much different from table sugar (that is, it isn't particularly high in nutrients), there are four good reasons to use it instead of sugar whenever possible. First, honey is twice as sweet as refined sugar, so you can use less of it. Second, it adds moisture to muffins, so you can use less fat. Third, honey's sweetness comes from sugars that are absorbed into the body more slowly than table or brown sugar, providing a steady supply of energy. And fourth, when purchased from non-commercial sources, honey is a natural and unprocessed food.

I buy my honey from a local beekeeper who sells to markets around town and throughout the county. He takes a lot of pride in his bees and the honey they produce. An expert, he knows that the taste, color, and texture of the honey changes with the seasons according to what the bees are attracted to at the time. Buying from a local supplier such as this assures that the honey is fresh and unprocessed.

You can store honey in your cupboard. This keeps it at room temperature—ideal for muffin making. But if you refrigerate your honey, I recommend warming it a little before mixing it with the other wet ingredients. Warming facilitates blending, especially when the honey is thick and cold, or when the wet ingredients are cold. To warm your honey (the kind that comes from bees, that is), place the whole container in a bowl of hot water about fifteen minutes before each use; or place the measured amount in a glass cup or bowl and then heat it in the microwave for about fifteen seconds. Either warming method should do the trick.

Molasses

A friend of mine from the mountains of North Carolina says he was fifteen years old before he learned that the sweet brown syrup he poured all over his hot cereal and toast every morning was called "molasses" and not simply "lasses." That's because he and his seven brothers and sisters loved the syrup so much, it was constantly on the move around the breakfast table. "Can I please have some 'mow' lasses," one or another of them would cry out with their thick Southern drawl. And the "lasses" would be sent their way.

"Lasses" adds a certain gusto to the flavor of muffins. It is rich in energy-providing carbohydrates, as well as iron and potassium—two nutrients that are especially good for the heart. You can buy molasses in a range of flavors and intensities—from regular (probably the most popular), to robust (the flavor I like best), to the thick and dark blackstrap molasses (too intense and too thick for our purposes).

Maple Syrup

Is the price of real maple syrup coming down or is it just that my grocer now stocks a less-expensive brand? I had grown so accustomed to paying four or five dollars for a pint of maple syrup that I would hardly bat an eye when I grabbed it off the shelf. Lately, however, the price has been half that. Needless to say, the first time I noticed the lower price I checked the label to make sure the syrup was 100-percent pure maple. It was. I hope these lower prices are not a passing phenomenon.

There's nothing like real maple syrup, is there? Such a unique flavor. And so rich! Do you know that it takes up to fifty gallons of sap from maple trees to make only one gallon of syrup? Thanks, maple trees.

Sugar, White and Brown

I used to believe that commercial brands of brown sugar were better than using refined white sugar. However, except for the presence of a few trace elements, brown sugar is as low in nutritional value as white sugar. I use it, not so much because I imagine it to be better, I just like its flavor. What gives brown sugar its color and its distinctive flavor is molasses, an ingredient that gives muffins pizzazz. If your palate does not agree, feel free to substitute white sugar for the brown in my muffins.

Spices, Extracts, and Citrus Peel

My last sweet secret is to incorporate aromatic spices, extracts and flavorings, and the sweet zing of lemon and orange peel into my muffins. These ingredients have a way of making muffins taste light and sweet without added sweetener. (For instructions on preparing citrus peel, see page 22.)

You may be tempted to use commercial brands of orange and lemon peel found in the spice section of your local grocery store, but I don't recommend them. If you have ever used the real thing, you know why. Prepared commercial brands just don't have the oomph.

EGGS AND EGG PRODUCTS

Lots of people are cholesterol- and/or fat-watchers who want to eat foods that are low in both. So let me address the egg question.

While creating my recipes, I experimented, making muffins without eggs, using the whole egg, using egg whites only, and using cholesterol-free and fat-free egg products. Then I compared the results. Here's what I found.

When making muffins without eggs, with rare exceptions, I have not been pleased with the results. The egg serves two purposes in muffin batters: It participates in the rising action, and it helps glue the muffin together. If, however, you are on an egg-free diet, consider using cornstarch as an egg substitute. Two tablespoons of cornstarch that are sifted together with the dry ingredients behave like one whole egg.

One of the simplest ways to reduce the fat in muffins is to limit the use of whole eggs or to use only the whites. ("Don't bake until you add the whites of the eggs.") While I do not hesitate to state that you can feel free to use whole eggs and egg whites interchangeably (one whole egg is equal to two egg whites), there is no question that using only egg whites alters the texture of the final product. They aren't as moist or springy. Whipping the egg whites until they are nearly stiff before adding them to your muffin batter can diminish that difference. (See "Whip the Eggs First, If You Like" on page 25.)

While there are a number of fat- and cholesterol-free egg products that may be attractive for one reason or another, I can't, in good conscience, recommend them for muffin making. For one thing, most of these products are egg whites with coloring agents, thickeners, and preservatives. In other words, they are not really food as we have come to appreciate it.

Why use a product that adds unwanted additives if you don't have to? Besides, I've found that muffins made with such products tend to be tough and rubbery. I don't like that. Prepared egg products might be easy to use, but they do not yield muffins that meet my high standards.

After all my experimenting, I have to admit that muffins simply come out better when they are made with whole eggs—especially recipes that use fruit or vegetable purées. Besides, the egg protein contained in the yolk seems to hold muffins together better.

Interestingly, using the whole egg does not appreciably affect the fat content of each muffin. It does, however, increase the cholesterol from 0 milligrams to about 18 milligrams. The USDA recommends that our daily intake of cholesterol not exceed 300 milligrams (one egg contains about 220 milligrams). It is easy to see that at 18 to 20 milligrams of cholesterol per muffin, one could eat quite a few before exceeding the limit.

SHORTENING

What to do about shortening? Do we use butter, margarine, or oil? How do we know which kinds are the best? How much is too much? How much is not enough? These are not easy questions to answer.

As Americans, we have the dubious distinction of enjoying the highest level of cardiovascular disease (particularly heart attacks and strokes) than any other country on the planet. Many have comparatively high levels of blood cholesterol due to an excessive consumption of saturated fat. To minimize the saturated fat content, I use canola oil in most of my sweet muffins, and olive or canola oil in my savory muffins. Of all the commonly used cooking oils, these are among the lowest in saturated fat. Safflower, soybean, corn, and sunflower oils have comparably low levels, too, so use them if you prefer.

If you love the flavor of butter or margarine, cannot imagine baked goods without them, and can afford the saturated fat in your diet, substitute butter or margarine for the oils I have suggested. One cup of oil equals one cup of melted butter or margarine. But if you want to keep your intake of saturated fat to a minimum, stick with the oils and avoid spreading butter or margarine on the final product.

All of the muffins in Chapter 7, "Low-Fat-and-Still-Yummy Muffins," contain 3 grams of fat or less. Such results are not possible without keeping a tight rein on the shortening. As you will see, many of these muffins contain no oil at all, and those that do call for only one tablespoon. I use no butter for the muffins in this chapter; margarine is used only in those recipes that contain crumble toppings and glazes. If you want to use more oil in these low-fat muffins, add canola oil to sweet muffins or olive oil to the savory ones. For each tablespoon of added oil, the fat content will increase by a little more than one gram per muffin. So, for example, if you add a $\frac{1}{4}$ cup of canola oil (4 tablespoons) to a recipe, each muffin will contain approximately four to five more grams of fat. When adding oil, you will also have to adjust the other liquids accordingly.

Finally, I do not use fat-free margarines or spreads, nor do I recommend their use in muffins. I say this without reservation. I have made many attempts to create quality muffins using fat-free margarines in the batter itself, but the results were consistently rubbery and tough. I have also tried using them to make crumble toppings and glazes. Without exception, fat-free margarine turned the crumble toppings into mush and the glazes into watery soup. Fat-free margarines simply do not contain the properties necessary for successful muffin making.

MILK

If you are a strict vegetarian, you will be pleased to know that you can substitute soy milk for the cow's milk in all my recipes. If you decide to use soy milk, there are a few things you should know.

Much of the packaged soy milk on the market is expensive and contains vanilla, cane juice, and barley malt or similar extras. These are added to reduce the soy milk's chalky flavor, making it more palatable to drink as a beverage. But for baking, you don't need these more expensive varieties. Plain old unflavored soy milk will do. It's not as costly and doesn't have any added flavors, so it is actually more desirable for baking.

I mix my own soy milk from packaged powder, which is available at your local heath food store and most grocery stores. There are several brands on the market, each with mixing directions clearly stated on the package.

Many of my recipes call for buttermilk— truly a miracle ingredient. A tad acidic, buttermilk gives the rising agents a boost (you can often see the muffins beginning to rise even before putting them in the oven). And buttermilk lends its thick, creamy texture to whatever ingredients it meets; it gives muffins a light, biscuit-like quality. Despite the fact that it has little or no fat (you can buy both low-fat and nonfat varieties) and comparatively little cholesterol (see Table 1.2, "Nutrient Analysis of Milk Varieties," below), buttermilk, when used in muffins, reduces the need for oil. It is also low in calories and loaded with calcium and protein. See what I mean about buttermilk being a miracle ingredient?

In the good old days when people would churn their own butter, buttermilk was truly buttermilk. That is, it was a byproduct of the butter-making process. Traditionally, one would churn sour milk until the fatty component—butter—solidified. What remained was a liquid residue that often contained some flecks of butter. Depending on how well it was strained, the buttermilk would be either very low in fat or completely fat free. Because it was made from sour milk, which made it easier for the butter to solidify, the buttermilk had a tangy or outright sour flavor.

Today, if you want authentic buttermilk, you would probably have to make your own butter—or make friends with someone who does! Adding bacterial cultures to low-fat or skim milk produces virtually all the buttermilk marketed today. The process, much like the yogurt-making process, produces lactic acid and acidophilus bacteria. This makes buttermilk more easily digested by people who are lactose intolerant.

TABLE 1.2 NUTRIENT ANALYSIS OF MILK VARIETIES					
Milk Type (8-ounce serving)	Total Calories	Fat grams	Cholesterol mgs	Protein grams	Calcium mgs
Buttermilk, Nonfat	90	0	5	9	250
Buttermilk, Low Fat	99	2	9	9	285
Milk, Skim	86	< 1	4	8	302
Milk, 1%	102	3	10	8	300
Milk, 2%	121	5	18	8	297
Milk, Whole	150	8	33	8	291

TOOLS AND UTENSILS

Setting up the kitchen to bake muffins is like getting ready for a Sunday stroll in the park—you don't need much by way of supplies. Just a few simple tools and utensils, a minimal exertion of energy, and you are ready for a good time.

FOOD PROCESSOR

I've always been slow to embrace new fashions (maybe even a little hard-headed), but when I come around, I'm like a religious convert. When I was a freshman in college, for example, and student government eliminated the dress code, I swore I'd never wear jeans to class. Three months later, mine were the most torn, patched, and jewel-studded jeans on campus.

I took to food processors in the same way. "Not me," I said, "I want to *feel* the food *I'm* chopping. It's strictly low tech for me." Years later, I find I can't live without my food processor. It's such a nifty little gadget. It blends, chops, grates, and pulverizes just about anything I feed it. If I feel weary or out of sorts, it smiles empathetically and says, "Let me do it

for you, Sweetie." I smile back gratefully and turn over the goods.

You will notice that most of my muffins are chock full of "goodies" (yummy little additions that make each muffin unique). My food processor helps me prepare these goodies. It chops nuts and seeds, and grates vegetables, ginger, and citrus peel. Sometimes I use my food processor to blend together a recipes's wet ingredients. If you think you will be baking a lot of muffins and you do not own a food processor, I strongly recommend that you get one. You'll be glad you did.

BOWLS AND SUCH

You'll need a few standard utensils—measuring cups, measuring spoons, and mixing bowls in assorted sizes. For muffins that call for veggies or fruit, you'll need a chopping surface and a sharp knife or two. A large wooden spoon is ideal for combining the wet and dry ingredients and acts as an accurate measure for spooning the batter into the muffin tins.

If you do not have a food processor, use your favorite chopping and grating utensils to prepare veggies, fruits, and nuts. Utensils such as a potato ricer (for mashing) and a hand-operated grinder (for chopping and grinding nuts and/or spices) also come in handy. You'll need a wire whisk to beat eggs and mix the other wet ingredients, and a hand-held grater to grate veggies.

Another important utensil for making successful muffins is a sifter. Despite what people say, whole grain muffins *can* be relatively light and airy. One of the secrets is to sift the flour once or twice before combining it with the wet ingredients. Sifting also eliminates the clumps that are often found in baking powder, baking soda, and whole grain flours.

Discover the value of sifting by conducting the following simple experiment. Take a cup of whole wheat or whole wheat pastry flour and sift it two times, measuring before and after each sifting. It grows, doesn't it? A cup of flour becomes $1\frac{1}{8}$ or even $1\frac{1}{4}$ cups! You see what sifting does? It fluffs the flour, kind of like whipping cream, and that fluffiness is passed on to the final product.

"But I don't like sifting," you whine. I know. I know. But if you don't listen to me on this one, you will have to find out the hard way. And you will have to put up with the tentative accolades of your friends and relations who haven't the heart to tell you that your whole grain masterpieces weigh a ton. It's eas-ier just to follow my suggestion. Get yourself a sifter. Okay?

MUFFIN TINS

Unless otherwise indicated, all the recipes in this book yield a dozen muffins and require three-inch muffin tins. It makes little difference if you use tin, iron, or no-stick pans. Baking time will be about the same for each. If, however, you use mini or jumbo muffin tins, you will have to adjust the baking time according-ly. A standard recipe for a dozen muffins makes about three dozen mini-muffins and requires approximately ten to fifteen minutes baking time. The same recipe yields six jumbo muffins and requires about twenty to twenty-five minutes baking time. If you want to get fancy and use heart-shaped, shell-shaped, or some other unusual-shaped tins, you will have to adjust the baking time accordingly. Read the manufacturer's suggestions and be willing to experiment a little. Your best bet is to watch your muffins closely as they bake.

BAKING CUPS

Here are the pros and cons on baking cups. You can avoid the use of butter, margarine, or oil, and cut down on cleanup time by using foil or paper baking cups. That's the good news. The bad news is that warm muffins tend to adhere to the baking cups. Often, after you peel away the paper, what's left is a crumbled core about the size of a donut hole. Very disappointing. You are likely to end up giving the muffin-coated paper to the dog and wondering if it was worth the effort.

There *is* a way out. You can reduce the cling factor by cooling the muffins completely before you gobble them up. "But," you say, "who wants to wait for them to cool?"

Admittedly, it's a dilemma. I tend not to use baking cups for this reason. If you use foil baking cups, remember that you won't be able to reheat the muffins in a microwave oven (or feed the muffin-coated paper to the dog). This could be a factor if you plan to freeze your muffins for later use. (See "Freezing and Reheating" on page 28).

TIPS AND TECHNIQUES

When I sat down to write about the techniques of muffin making, I thought I would have only a few tips to share. I mean muffins are so easy to make, how much is there to say? I soon realized, however, that lots of little details lie behind every successful batch. And these are the very tidbits of information that help make muffin baking a breeze.

GET THE INGREDIENTS READY BEFOREHAND

Before you start, it's a good idea to double-check your supplies and make certain that you have everything you will need—especially the standard ingredients. One time, I went to the grocery store three times just to bake two batches of muffins because I assumed I had the basics when I didn't.

Read the recipe to see if any of the ingredients call for special preparations. For example, one recipe might call for chopped roasted walnuts; another, grated orange peel. If you prepare these ingredients first and set them aside, the recipe will come together quickly and easily. You'll find the following tips helpful:

❏ **Preparing Citrus Peel and Ginger Root.** Orange peel, lemon peel, and ginger root can be grated in batches in your food processor and then stored in the refrigerator for several weeks.

Peel an orange or lemon, remove most of the pith, and chop the rind into $\frac{1}{2}$-inch bits. Process the rind in the food processor using the purée blade until it resembles coarse meal. For ginger root, remove the tough outer skin and chop the ginger into 1-inch bits. Using the purée blade of a food processor, chop the ginger into fine pieces. I find four-ounce plastic containers with lids perfect for storing these ingredients. I use an orange-colored container for orange peel, yellow for the lemon, and brown for the ginger root. Then, whenever I am mixing up a batch of muffins that calls for one of these ingredients, I simply reach into the refrigerator and grab the right colored container.

❏ **Preparing Nuts.** Whenever I buy nuts, like walnuts, almonds, or pecans, I roast them right away if they aren't roasted already. I place them in a single layer on an ungreased baking sheet, then pop them into a 275°F oven for about twenty minutes. As the nuts roast, I stir them occasionally so they don't burn. After cooling the nuts to room temperature, I coarsely chop them in my food processor, place them in one-quart canning jars, and store them in the back of the refrigerator's bottom shelf—the dead zone, as I call it. What else can you put

back there but things that you don't use every day? Again, I prepare the nuts so they are ready to grab whenever I need them.

❏ **Preparing Banana Purée.** Does your grocery store sell ripe bananas at reduced prices? Mine, too. When this happens I buy several pounds, then I purée and freeze them for future use. I do so according to the quantities I need for my favorite muffin recipes—and I suggest you do, too. For example, both my Better Banana Nut Bran Muffins and Bananas Foster Muffins call for three ripe bananas. Friends-of-the-Earth Vegan Muffins call for two, and my Tropical Fruit Muffins call for only one. I purée one or two bananas and freeze them in recycled eight-ounce margarine tubs; I put three puréed bananas in pint-size yogurt containers. (Of course, I label the containers with the contents and amount.) Stored this way, the purée will keep up to three months. When I want to bake banana muffins, all I have to do is defrost the container with the desired amount of purée.

❏ **Preparing Crystallized Ginger and Dried Fruits.** When it comes to chopping crystallized ginger and dried fruit, you will have to use your judgment in determining the best method. You can chop crystallized ginger in the food processor, but it must be done gently. If you process too hard or for too long, the ginger will become a paste. If the ginger is particularly fresh or soft, I don't recommend this method. Chop it by hand instead. The same holds true for dried fruits. Sticky dried fruits like prunes, figs, and dates are better chopped by hand. Dried apricots that are moist should be chopped by hand as well. Dried apples, peaches, and pears can be chopped in the food processor. Of course, pea-sized fruits such as raisins, cranberries, and raspberries don't need to be chopped at all.

❏ **Preparing Crumble Toppings.** It seems that everybody loves muffins with crumble toppings, but nobody wants to take the time to prepare the crumble. I hope I've made it easy for you—just follow the directions with each recipe. But here's an added tip: Put the crumble ingredients in a medium-sized bowl, slip a tape or CD into the player, and sit yourself down on a barstool or chair in the kitchen. Then, with a pastry blender or two knives, cut the margarine into the dry ingredients until the crumble is the consistency you want. It'll take only a song or two. Your choice of music, however, is extremely important in determining the success or failure of your crumble topping. I choose songs from Eric Clapton's *Unplugged,*

Simon and Garfunkel's *Concert in the Park,* Van Morrison's *Moondance,* or anything by Peter, Paul and Mary. You choose whatever music turns you on.

SIFT THE DRY INGREDIENTS

Sifting is very important, but some people never got into the habit of sifting. I guess it's like flossing your teeth. If you don't develop the habit early in life, you may never do so. When you don't sift, little clumps of baking soda or baking powder can ruin the flavor of your muffins. The only way to avoid this is to *sift, sift, sift.* Sifting also fluffs the flour, making the final muffin product lighter. So do it.

ADD THE GOODIES AS INSTRUCTED

Some of my recipe instructions have you adding the goodies to the dry ingredients, while other recipes tell you to add them to the wet ingredients. My general rule of thumb is as follows: I add fresh fruits like apples or blueberries, or sticky dried fruits such as prunes or figs, to the dry ingredients and then toss to coat. This does two things. It prevents these goodies from bleeding into the rest of the muffin, causing an unattractive and often gooey effect. It also helps keep them from sinking to the bottom of the cup.

By contrast, I add small dried fruits, such as raisins or cranberries, to the wet ingredients and stir to combine. This helps plump the dried goodies a little before baking and prevents the flour from collecting in the nooks and crannies, the wrinkles and crevices. And for the sake of convenience, when a recipe has both fresh and dried fruits in the goody list, I add them all to the dry ingredients.

STIR THE DRY AND WET INGREDIENTS TOGETHER AS LITTLE AS POSSIBLE

When wheat flour is combined with a wet ingredient, and then kneaded or stirred, a protein called *gluten* forms. Gluten causes the mixture to become sticky and take on an elastic quality. This is why wheat flour is so suitable for making breads. By kneading the dough, we encourage the gluten to form, resulting in that spongy quality we like so much in bread.

But muffins are another matter. We don't want them to have that spongy texture, so we work to prevent the gluten from forming. We do this by stirring muffin batter as little as possible. This is why I emphasize preparing the wet ingredients and dry ingredients separately before combining them. Thus, the final mixing can be kept to minimum.

WHIP THE EGGS FIRST, IF YOU LIKE

As discussed in "Eggs and Egg Products," beginning on page 16, feel free to use one whole egg or two egg whites interchangeably in any of my muffin recipes. All instructions have you blend the egg or egg whites with the remaining wet ingredients. However, you can pump up the volume (and the rising power) of an egg by whipping it before adding it to the batter. Here's how. Before blending the wet ingredients, whip the whole egg or egg whites in a food processor for about fifteen seconds. The whole egg will become lighter in color and increase slightly in volume. Egg whites will become milky and start to stiffen. After whipping, add the remaining wet ingredients to the food processor and pulse to blend. Then you can proceed with the recipe. If you do not have a food processor, use a wire whisk to bring about similar results.

Keep in mind that this is an optional step. If you are in a hurry, it is not necessary to whip the whole egg or the egg whites separately.

However, if you have the time, do it. It will improve the texture of the finished product.

MAKE ONLY ONE BATCH OF MUFFINS AT A TIME

One is often tempted to double the ingredients of a muffin recipe and make more than one batch at a time. This is an especially attractive idea if you need to bake several dozen muffins and freeze some for later use. While this may seem like a good idea, I don't think you will be happy with the results. Larger batches seem to require more mixing, which compromises the muffins' light texture. I have a rule. Never mix more than one batch at a time. If you have a large oven and want to bake more than one batch at a time, fine. But mix the individual batches separately. Trust me. You will be happier with the results.

USE NONSTICK COOKING SPRAY ON MUFFIN TINS

I used to take a hard line on nonstick cooking sprays to grease my muffin tins. I didn't like the taste they left on my muffins. In addition, I felt they left a residue on the muffin tins that was difficult to remove. Well, I took some flack for my position from both friends and family alike. They have convinced me that nonstick cooking sprays have improved enough over the years to warrant their use in muffin making. Besides, cooking sprays sure are convenient to use!

Before filling the cups with batter, I spray the ten cups around the perimeter of a twelve-cup tin and fill them with batter first. Then, if there is still more batter, I spray and fill the remaining cups as needed. This saves your tin from turning black from baked-on grease. Of course, you can also spray all twelve cups and then wipe the unused ones with a paper towel before baking.

FILL THE MUFFIN TINS

I like a full, dome-shaped muffin. For this reason, I fill my muffin cups nearly to the top with batter. The batter should show its head a little above the rim of each cup. Remember that whole-grain muffins do not rise as much as muffins made from refined products, so don't hesitate to fill those tins. Then, in the rising they will spread out over the edge of the cup. This makes for a nice large muffin with a mushroom-like cap. I like this effect. If you prefer muffins that peak in the middle, fill the muffin cups two-thirds full. Each recipe will then produce more than the specified yield.

Be sure to fill each cup evenly. If for any reason you do not use all twelve cups, fill the empty ones halfway with water. This allows for even baking of the remaining muffins. You may want to make the exact number of muffins the recipe says it should yield, but even slight variations in measuring, in the size of muffin tins, or in the way you prepare the batter can change the yield. It is better to fill each baking cup according to the instructions and make one more or one less muffin, than to try to ensure that each batch yields exactly twelve.

If you have a large oven and plenty of tins, you may want to try the following method: Rather than filling every cup in a twelve-muffin tin, use two tins and fill every other cup with batter. For this method, you won't need to fill the empty cups with water as previously suggested. This method enhances the quick rising action that is so necessary for successful muffins.

OVEN TEMPERATURE

Always be sure to preheat the oven at least ten minutes before baking your muffins. The rising action must be quick and to the point, so preheating is essential. Center the muffin tin on a rack placed in the middle of the oven and, unless instructed otherwise, bake each batch for fifteen to twenty minutes at 400°F. (Batters with large amounts of fruit tend to burn at this temperature, so they should bake in a slightly cooler oven.) If your oven has a glass door, watching the muffins bake can be particularly exciting. I like to sit by the oven door and watch my muffins blossom. It's kind of like watching an amaryllis bloom!

If you don't pay proper attention to the oven temperature, your muffins will be topsy-turvy affairs. If you've ever baked muffins that look like flying saucers or the Leaning Tower of Pisa, you know what I mean. It means the oven was either too cool or too hot. As seen in Figure 1.1 on page 28, when the oven is too hot, the muffins will have uneven peaks that resemble chefs' hats that are leaning to one side. When the oven temperature is too cool, the muffins will be flat in the middle. If you are consistently having problems, check your oven's thermostat.

For best results when baking more than a dozen muffins at a time, bake each batch separately. If this is not possible and you need to bake more than one batch at a time, place the muffins tins side-by-side in the middle of the oven. If your oven is not wide enough to place the muffin tins side by side, place one above the other, but switch and turn the tins when the muffins are half-baked.

ARE THEY DONE YET?

When the smell of fresh-baked muffins fills the kitchen, your muffins are done. Yum-O! But let's get down to details. The muffins are done when they are fully cooked in the center. You can usually tell just by looking at them. If you are not sure, press the center of one or two muffins. If they are not overly moist and spring back after you apply pressure, they are fully cooked. You can also test by inserting a toothpick in the center of one or two muffins. If the toothpick comes out clean (without wet or moist batter clinging to it), your muffins are done.

Figure 1.1. Effect of Oven Temperature on Muffins. Correctly baked muffins will be straight-sided and slightly rounded on top (left). Flat muffins result when the oven temperature is too low (center). An oven that is too hot causes muffins to have uneven peaks (right).

COOL BEFORE REMOVING FROM THE TIN

Be sure to wait ten minutes before removing the muffins from their tins. The wait can be difficult—especially when you are hungry. Muffin making cultivates patience.

If you grease the tins generously before baking and allow the muffins to cool at least ten minutes, a gentle twist of the noggin (theirs, not yours) will free them easily. If you try to force them out of the baking cups before they cool, you may need the assistance of a knife or fork, and the hot muffins are likely to break apart. Plus, you run the risk of scratching your tins. Be patient. This step is especially important if the tin is Teflon coated or has another fancy finish that can be scraped off and consumed.

FREEZING AND REHEATING

Sometimes I bake muffins just for the fun of it and freeze them for later use. Then if there is a last-minute need, or if I get up too late to make a batch for breakfast, I can grab as many muffins as I need and reheat them in a flash.

If you want to freeze muffins for later use, simply wrap each one securely in plastic wrap and place it in a zip-lock bag. Four muffins fit nicely in a one-quart bag; nine, in a gallon bag. I use half-inch labels to mark each muffin before freezing. Once frozen, most muffins look alike! Wrapped this way, muffins will keep for up to three months in the freezer.

Be sure to cool your muffins completely before wrapping and freezing them. If they are still warm, ice crystals will form inside the wrapper and your muffins will become gooey as they thaw.

To reheat frozen muffins, simply place them—wrapper and all—in a microwave oven on high for thirty to fifty seconds (time varies with each oven).

READY, SET, GO!

You are now armed with everything you need to create an exquisite array of delectable, satisfying muffins. You know the best ingredients, the right tools and equipment, and the proper techniques for ensuring muffin success every time. With minimum fuss, you can bake up a batch in a snap to enjoy any time of the day. Mmm. I'm getting hungry just thinking about it. Come on. It's time to get started.

2. Get-Up-and-Go Muffins

All happiness depends on a leisurely breakfast.

—JOHN GUNTHER, WRITER

I had a hard time waking up this morning. A thick fog clouded my mind as I stumbled to the bathroom. When I looked in the mirror through dilated eyes, the face looking back could barely see me. "I need a pot of coffee," I said to myself.

After groping my way back to the kitchen, I grabbed the bag of coffee beans (Nicaraguan something-or-other) that my friend Douglas had given me, filled the coffee grinder nearly to the top, put the lid in place, and depressed the lever. Nothing happened.

"Hmm." I could scarcely think my way through this one. I checked the electrical connection. It seemed to be okay. I pushed the lever again. Still nothing. Not knowing if the problem was the connecting lever or the switch itself, I decided to try depressing the switch with a shish kabob skewer to see if I could start the machine that way. I suppose I should mention that I neglected to remove the beans from the grinder before doing so. The blades whirred and the centrifugal force sent coffee beans in various stages of grind all over the kitchen. There were beans in the opened drawers, in the sink, on the windowsill, in my eyes, and on the floor four feet away. Later, I even found some in my pockets. The machine itself was empty.

"This isn't working," I thought. I need to wake up before I tackle complex life functions. I sat down on the couch with the basket of muffins I had baked the night before—Better Banana Nut Bran Muffins. I unwrapped one, bit into it, and BOING. It was like pressing the "open" switch of an automatic garage door opener. The flavors of bananas and nuts consumed my attention and suddenly the fog that had clouded my awareness lifted. "Ah, yes," I thought. "I remember this. This is morning."

I had morning in mind when I created my "Get-Up-and-Go Muffins." Their rich flavors and textures will get your attention every time and help you start your day with a little vitality and awareness—not to mention a smile. But don't limit yourself to enjoying these muffins only for breakfast. They're great any time of night or day.

Apple-Orange-Oat Bran Muffins

I created these muffins for people who want to increase the amount of oat bran in their diets. The orange peel provides a light flavor and the apple-sauce, a natural sweetness. If you find that these muffins are sweet enough without the brown sugar, feel free to leave it out. Apple-Orange-Oat Bran Muffins are both crowd-pleasing and nutritious.

1. Preheat the oven to 375°F.

2. Sift together all the dry ingredients, except the oat bran, in a large bowl. Add the oat bran and stir to combine. Add the goodies and toss to coat.

3. Whisk the wet ingredients in a medium bowl.

4. Pour the wet ingredients into the dry mixture. Stir just until mixed. *Do not overstir.*

5. Spoon the batter into a greased or papered muffin tin. Fill each cup nearly to the top.

6. Bake for 15 to 20 minutes.

7. Cool the muffins at least 10 minutes before removing from the tin.

DRY INGREDIENTS

1 cup unbleached white flour

1 cup whole wheat flour

$1/4$ cup light brown sugar

$1 1/2$ teaspoons baking powder

1 teaspoon baking soda

$3/4$ teaspoon ground cinnamon

$3/4$ teaspoon ground nutmeg

1 cup oat bran

WET INGREDIENTS

$1 1/2$ cups applesauce

1 cup milk

1 large egg

1 tablespoon grated orange peel

1 teaspoon vanilla extract

GOODIES

$3/4$ cup chopped apples

YIELD
12
MUFFINS

DRY INGREDIENTS

I cup unbleached white flour

$^1/_2$ cup whole wheat flour

$^3/_4$ cup light brown sugar

I teaspoon baking powder

I teaspoon baking soda

$^1/_4$ teaspoon sea salt

I cup wheat bran

WET INGREDIENTS

3 ripe bananas, mashed (I $^1/_2$ cups)

$^3/_4$ cup water

I large egg

I $^1/_2$ teaspoons vanilla extract

I teaspoon grated lemon peel

GOODIES

$^3/_4$ cup chopped roasted walnuts

Better Banana Nut Bran Muffins

Bananas are great. But have you ever had banana "anything" that had enough bananas in it? Me neither. That's why I created this recipe, which calls for three ripe bananas! How do you know when they're ripe enough? As bananas ripen, brown specks appear on the peel. When overripe, they're completely brown. For baking, they should be past "just ripe" and not quite overripe. They will be sweet, but not too sweet, and moist without being gooey. Hey, did you know that the banana is a berry? The largest on earth!

1. Preheat the oven to 375°F.

2. Sift all the dry ingredients, except the wheat bran, together in a large bowl. Add the bran and the walnuts and stir to combine.

3. Whisk the wet ingredients in a medium bowl or blend in a food processor. Pour the wet ingredients into the dry mixture. Stir just until mixed. *Do not overstir.*

4. Spoon the batter into a greased or papered muffin tin. Fill each cup nearly to the top.

5. Bake for 15 to 20 minutes.

6. Cool the muffins at least 10 minutes before removing from the tin.

Blueberry Blintz Muffins

YIELD
12
MUFFINS

Blueberries have a way of sinking to the bottom of muffin cups and sticking to the tin. You can, however, avoid this not-so-calamitous calamity. First, make sure the batter is nice and thick. That's one of the things I like about these muffins—the ricotta cheese and sour cream result in a substantial batter. Second, allow them to cool a little longer than most muffins before removing them from the tin, about 15 to 20 minutes.

1. Preheat the oven to 375°F.

2. Measure and sift the dry ingredients together in a large bowl. Add the goodies and toss to coat.

3. Whisk the wet ingredients in a medium bowl. Do not use a blender or food processor.

4. Pour the wet ingredients into the dry mixture. Stir just until mixed. *Do not overstir.*

5. Spoon the batter into a greased or papered muffin tin. Fill each cup nearly to the top.

6. Bake for 15 to 20 minutes.

7. Cool the muffins at least 15 to 20 minutes before removing from the tin.

DRY INGREDIENTS

1 cup whole wheat pastry flour

1 cup whole wheat flour

1/4 cup oat flour

2 teaspoons baking powder

1 teaspoon baking soda

1/4 teaspoon sea salt

WET INGREDIENTS

3/4 cup ricotta cheese

1/2 cup sour cream

1 cup milk

1/4 cup canola oil

1 large egg

1/2 cup honey

2 teaspoons grated lemon peel

GOODIES

1 1/4 cups firm fresh blueberries, washed and patted dry

YIELD
12
MUFFINS

DRY INGREDIENTS

1 cup unbleached white flour

3/4 cup whole wheat flour

3/4 cup yellow or blue cornmeal

2 teaspoons baking powder

1 teaspoon baking soda

1/4 teaspoon sea salt

WET INGREDIENTS

1 cup milk

1/2 cup applesauce

1/2 cup blueberry or grape all-fruit jam

1/4 cup canola oil

1 large egg

1 teaspoon vanilla extract

GOODIES

1 1/4 cups firm fresh blueberries, washed and patted dry

3/4 cup coconut

Blue Morning Muffins

I value restraint. Once in a while, I think it's good to say no to those gimme, gimme, gimme thoughts that pop into my head. If this is beginning to sound like an apology, it's because it is. You see, I feel a little guilty for not holding back the impulse to add coconut to these muffins—what with the added fat and all. But I think you will agree that the combination of blueberries, cornmeal, and coconut is a great one! If you are on a low-fat diet, simply eliminate the coconut.

1. Preheat the oven to 375°F.

2. Sift all the dry ingredients together in a large bowl. Add the coconut and stir to combine. Add the blueberries and toss to coat.

3. Whisk the wet ingredients in a medium bowl or blend in a food processor.

4. Pour the wet ingredients into the dry mixture. Stir just until mixed. *Do not overstir.*

5. Spoon the batter into a greased or papered muffin tin. Fill each cup nearly to the top.

6. Bake for 15 to 20 minutes.

7. Cool the muffins at least 15 to 20 minutes before removing from the tin.

Breakfast Boston Brown Muffins

DRY INGREDIENTS

1 cup whole wheat
pastry flour

$1/2$ cup unbleached
white flour

$1/2$ cup buckwheat flour

$1/4$ cup yellow cornmeal

$1/2$ cup light brown sugar

$1 1/2$ teaspoons baking
powder

1 teaspoon baking soda

$1/4$ teaspoon sea salt

WET INGREDIENTS

$1 1/2$ cups buttermilk

$1/2$ cup apple juice
concentrate

$1/4$ cup canola oil

1 large egg

GOODIES

1 cup raisins

1 cup roasted sunflower
seeds

These are one of my most favorite morning muffins. When I eat one, perhaps with a bit of fruit or fruit juice and a cup of coffee, I'm ready for just about anything. Its fresh-baked whole grain goodness stays with me all morning, supplying much-needed energy as it slowly digests in my system. Mmm. Mmm. Mmm. It tastes good. I feel good. Heck, I even look good. Try them with Maple Butter Spread (page 190).

1. Preheat the oven to 375°F.

2. Sift the dry ingredients together in a large bowl.

3. Whisk the wet ingredients in a medium bowl or blend in a food processor. Add the goodies and stir to combine.

4. Pour the wet mixture into the dry ingredients. Stir just until mixed. *Do not overstir.*

5. Spoon the batter into a greased or papered muffin tin. Fill each cup nearly to the top.

6. Bake for 15 to 20 minutes.

7. Cool the muffins at least 10 minutes before removing from the tin.

YIELD
11–12
MUFFINS

DRY INGREDIENTS

1 cup whole wheat flour

3/4 cup unbleached white flour

3/4 cup buckwheat flour

1 1/2 teaspoons baking soda

1 teaspoon baking powder

1/4 teaspoon sea salt

WET INGREDIENTS

1 cup buttermilk

1 cup maple syrup

1 large egg

1 teaspoon grated orange peel

GOODIES

3/4 cup firm fresh blueberries, washed and patted dry

Buckwheat Buttermilk Muffins with Blueberries and Maple Syrup

I had heard that the pancakes at Mabry Mill were incredible. But what was so special about those particular pancakes, served at that particular restaurant, located in the mountains of North Carolina? I had to find out, so a friend and I went on a quest to discover the answer. Wow! The pancakes were to-die-for! What can I say? That's how muffins are born.

1. Preheat the oven to 400°F.

2. Sift the dry ingredients together in a large bowl. Add the blueberries and toss to coat.

3. Whisk the wet ingredients in a medium bowl or blend in a food processor. Pour the wet ingredients into the dry mixture. Stir just until mixed. *Do not overstir.*

4. Spoon the batter into a greased or papered muffin tin. Fill each cup nearly to the top.

5. Bake for 15 to 20 minutes.

6. Cool the muffins at least 15 to 20 minutes before removing from the tin.

California Mix Muffins

YIELD
12
MUFFINS

For those who have never heard of it, California mix is a glorious combination of dried fruits and nuts—usually raisins, dates, apricots, pineapple, papaya, banana, coconut, pumpkin seeds, walnuts, pecans, almonds, and Brazil nuts. It's available at health food stores and commercial markets. And does it make wonderful muffins! The pieces of fruit and nuts in this mix are often too large for muffins, so you'll have to chop them first.

1. Preheat the oven to 400°F.

2. Sift the dry ingredients together in a large bowl.

3. Whisk the wet ingredients in a medium bowl or blend in a food processor. Add the goodies and stir to combine.

4. Pour the wet mixture into the dry ingredients. Stir just until mixed. *Do not overstir.*

5. Spoon the batter into a greased or papered muffin tin. Fill each cup nearly to the top.

6. Bake for 15 to 20 minutes.

7. Cool the muffins at least 10 minutes before removing from the tin.

DRY INGREDIENTS

1 $\frac{1}{2}$ cups whole wheat pastry flour

$\frac{1}{2}$ cup whole wheat flour

$\frac{1}{2}$ cup unbleached white flour

$\frac{1}{2}$ cup light brown sugar

2 teaspoons baking powder

1 teaspoon baking soda

WET INGREDIENTS

1 ripe banana, mashed ($\frac{1}{2}$ cup)

1 $\frac{1}{4}$ cups milk

$\frac{1}{4}$ cup canola oil

1 large egg

1 tablespoon grated lemon peel

2 teaspoons vanilla extract

GOODIES

1 $\frac{1}{2}$ cups coarsely chopped California mix

Catherine's Lemon-Red Raspberry Muffins

**YIELD
11–12
MUFFINS**

DRY INGREDIENTS

1 cup whole wheat pastry flour

1 cup unbleached white flour

$1/2$ cup whole wheat flour

$1/2$ cup sugar

$1 1/2$ teaspoons baking powder

1 teaspoon baking soda

$1/4$ teaspoon sea salt

WET INGREDIENTS

$3/4$ cup buttermilk

$1/2$ cup applesauce

$1/2$ cup honey

$1/4$ cup canola oil

1 large egg

$2 1/2$ tablespoons grated lemon peel

GOODIES

$3/4$ cup firm fresh raspberries, washed, patted dry, and halved

Niece Catherine, as I like to call her when she calls me Aunt Gloria, turned me on to the French fruit-shaped hard candies called pastilles. They are the ones that come in those small round tins. Very chic. The way Catherine twisted the lid and presented the tin before me reminded me of the way movie stars offered each other cigarettes in 1940's films. "Pastille?" "Oh, thank you, darling. Don't mind if I do." Lemon and raspberry are Catherine's favorites, and the inspiration for these muffins.

1. Preheat the oven to 375°F.

2. Measure and sift the dry ingredients together in a large bowl. Add the raspberries and toss to coat. (This will keep them from bleeding into the rest of the muffin.)

3. Whisk the wet ingredients in a medium bowl or blend in a food processor. Pour the wet mixture into the dry ingredients. Stir just until mixed, taking care not to break the raspberries or cause their juice to color the batter. *Do not overstir.*

4. Spoon the batter into a greased or papered muffin tin. Fill each cup nearly to the top.

5. Bake for 15 to 20 minutes.

6. Cool the muffins at least 15 to 20 minutes before removing from the tin.

Cherry Irish Soda Muffins

YIELD
12
MUFFINS

For this muffin, I've spruced up my sister Betty's traditional Irish soda bread recipe by adding dried cherries. The result? Unforgettable tasting muffins. They are unusual enough that they come to mind when I ask myself, "What could I have for breakfast that's really interesting?" Yet, they are ordinary enough that I always seem to have the ingredients on hand. These muffins are probably the most versatile ones I make—lending themselves well to any meal, any time of day.

1. Preheat the oven to 400°F.

2. Sift together all the dry ingredients, except the caraway seeds, in a large bowl. Add the caraway seeds and stir to combine.

3. Whisk the wet ingredients in a medium bowl or blend in a food processor. Add the cherries and currants, and stir to combine.

4. Pour the wet mixture into the dry ingredients. Stir just until mixed. *Do not overstir.*

5. Spoon the batter into a greased or papered muffin tin. Fill each cup nearly to the top.

6. Bake for 15 to 20 minutes.

7. Cool the muffins at least 10 minutes before removing from the tin.

DRY INGREDIENTS

1 1/2 cups unbleached white flour

1 cup whole wheat flour

1/4 cup light brown sugar

1 teaspoon baking powder

1 teaspoon baking soda

1/4 teaspoon sea salt

1 tablespoon caraway seeds

WET INGREDIENTS

1 1/4 cups buttermilk

1/2 cup water

1 large egg

1 tablespoon canola oil

1 tablespoon grated orange peel

1 tablespoon grated lemon peel

GOODIES

3/4 cup dried cherries

1/2 cup currants

Crazy Raisin Muffins

**YIELD
12
MUFFINS**

DRY INGREDIENTS

1 cup whole wheat
pastry flour

1 cup whole wheat flour

$1/2$ cup unbleached
white flour

$1 1/2$ teaspoons baking
powder

1 teaspoon baking soda

$1/4$ teaspoon sea salt

2 teaspoons ground
cloves

2 teaspoons ground
cinnamon

WET INGREDIENTS

$1 1/4$ cups milk

$1/4$ cup margarine or butter,
melted

1 large egg

GOODIES

2 cups raisins

2 teaspoon grated
orange peel

$1/4$ cup honey

1 cup boiling water

Years ago, there was a popular raisin cake recipe making the rounds in American kitchens. It called for mayonnaise, lots of raisins, and a hint of cloves. While the raisins were great, the cake was screaming for more cloves—and the mayonnaise had to go (too much cholesterol). I've transformed that recipe into these muffins. And just in case your sweet tooth is not quite satisfied with the natural sweetness of raisins, I've added a little honey to the pot. The bears and the bees love it . . . and so do I.

1. Place the raisins, orange peel, and honey in a medium bowl, and cover with the boiling water. Set aside to cool. The raisins will absorb the liquid and become plump.

2. Preheat the oven to 400°F.

3. Sift the dry ingredients together in a large bowl.

4. Whisk the wet ingredients in a medium bowl or blend in a food processor. Pour the wet ingredients into the raisin mixture and stir to combine. Add to the dry ingredients, and stir just until mixed. *Do not overstir.*

5. Spoon the batter into a greased or papered muffin tin. Fill each cup nearly to the top.

6. Bake for 15 to 20 minutes.

7. Cool the muffins at least 10 minutes before removing from the tin.

Crunchy Granola Crumble Muffins

I used to make my own granola, but these days I buy it ready-made at health food stores, food co-ops, open-air markets, and even my neighborhood grocery store. Today's granola comes in many flavors—almond, apple, maple, orange, and even blueberry and raspberry—and they are all very tasty. You can make these muffins with any flavor granola you like. No matter what brand or flavor I use, these muffins come out great every time.

1. Preheat the oven to 400°F.

2. To prepare the topping, grind the granola in a food processor or hand-operated grinder until it resembles coarse meal. Combine the granola, flours, and cinnamon in a medium bowl. Using a pastry blender or two knives, cut the margarine into the mixture to form crumbles. Set aside.

3. Sift together all the dry ingredients, except the granola, in a large bowl. Add the granola and stir to combine.

4. Whisk the wet ingredients in a medium bowl or blend in a food processor. Pour the wet ingredients into the dry ingredients. Stir just until mixed. *Do not overstir.*

5. Spoon the batter into a greased or papered muffin tin. Fill each cup nearly to the top. Top each cup of batter with the crumble topping, taking care to spread it evenly over each cup. Too much topping piled high in the middle will prevent the muffins from rising properly.

6. Bake for 15 to 20 minutes.

7. Cool the muffins at least 10 minutes before removing from the tin.

DRY INGREDIENTS

1 cup whole wheat flour

1 cup unbleached white flour

$1\frac{1}{2}$ teaspoons baking powder

$\frac{1}{2}$ teaspoon baking soda

$\frac{1}{2}$ teaspoon ground cinnamon

$\frac{1}{2}$ teaspoon ground nutmeg

$\frac{1}{4}$ teaspoon sea salt

1 cup granola

WET INGREDIENTS

$1\frac{1}{4}$ cups buttermilk

$\frac{1}{2}$ cup applesauce

$\frac{1}{2}$ cup maple syrup

1 large egg

2 teaspoons grated orange peel

1 teaspoon vanilla extract

CRUMBLE TOPPING

$\frac{1}{2}$ cup granola

2 tablespoons whole wheat flour

2 tablespoons unbleached white flour

$\frac{1}{8}$ teaspoon ground cinnamon

2 tablespoons margarine, softened

YIELD
12
MUFFINS

Eat-Your-Oatmeal Muffins

DRY INGREDIENTS

2 cups whole wheat pastry flour

1 1/2 teaspoons baking powder

1 teaspoon baking soda

1 teaspoon ground cinnamon

3/4 teaspoon ground ginger

1/4 teaspoon sea salt

3/4 cup rolled oats

WET INGREDIENTS

1 cup milk

1/2 cup apple juice concentrate

1/4 cup canola oil

1/4 cup honey

1 large egg

1 1/2 teaspoons vanilla extract

GOODIES

1 medium apple or pear (or both), chopped

1/2 cup raisins

1/2 cup roasted sunflower seeds

I love creamy oatmeal with a hint of spice and topped with chopped fruit, nuts, and raisins. Can you blame me for wanting to make a muffin that captures these flavors? For this recipe, I recommend using fresh apples or pears—they are almost always available and hold up beautifully in muffins. You needn't peel the fruit. Just scrub, core, quarter, and chop. These muffins taste like great big oatmeal cookies. Try them with Honey Cinnamon Spread (page 190) or Apple Butter Spread (page 189).

1. Preheat the oven to 400°F.

2. Sift the dry ingredients together in a large bowl. Add the goodies and toss to coat.

3. Whisk the wet ingredients in a medium bowl or blend in a food processor. Pour the wet ingredients into the dry mixture. Stir just until mixed. *Do not overstir.*

4. Spoon the batter into a greased or papered muffin tin. Fill each cup nearly to the top.

5. Bake for 15 to 20 minutes.

6. Cool the muffins at least 10 minutes before removing from the tin.

Fakin' Bacon Muffins

YIELD
10
MUFFINS

Fakin' bacon is a scrumptious way to enjoy the smoked flavor of bacon with none of the cholesterol, a fraction of the fat, about half the sodium, and, of course, no meat. Because it is made from tempeh (a cultured soybean and/or grain product), it is chock full of protein goodness. Look for it in your local health food store under a variety of names. The name fakin' bacon implies that it is imitation bacon. I prefer to think of it as real *smoked tempeh.*

DRY INGREDIENTS

1 ½ cups unbleached white flour

1 cup whole wheat flour

¼ cup millet flour

2 ½ teaspoons baking powder

WET INGREDIENTS

1 ¾ cups buttermilk

¼ cup canola oil

1 large egg

GOODIES

6- to 8-ounce package fakin' bacon

¼ cup chopped onion

1 tablespoon canola oil

1. Preheat the oven to 400°F.

2. In a small skillet over medium heat, sauté the fakin' bacon and onion in the canola oil until lightly browned. Set aside to cool.

3. Sift the dry ingredients together in a large bowl. Add the fakin' bacon and toss to coat. If necessary, crumble any large chunks of fakin' bacon.

4. Whisk the wet ingredients in a medium bowl or blend in a food processor. Pour the wet ingredients into the dry mixture. Stir just until mixed. *Do not overstir.*

5. Spoon the batter into a greased or papered muffin tin. Fill each cup nearly to the top.

6. Bake for 15 to 20 minutes.

7. Cool the muffins at least 10 minutes before removing from the tin.

YIELD
12
MUFFINS

DRY INGREDIENTS

1 $^3/_4$ cups whole wheat flour

$^3/_4$ cup whole wheat pastry flour

2 tablespoons cornstarch

1 $^1/_2$ teaspoons baking soda

1 teaspoon baking powder

1 teaspoon ground cinnamon

$^1/_4$ teaspoon ground mace

$^1/_4$ teaspoon sea salt

WET INGREDIENTS

2 ripe bananas, mashed (1 cup)

$^3/_4$ cup soy milk

$^1/_2$ cup honey

$^1/_4$ cup apple juice concentrate

1 tablespoon molasses

1 teaspoon vanilla extract

1 teaspoon grated lemon peel

GOODIES

$^1/_2$ cup coarsely chopped roasted walnuts

$^1/_4$ cup chopped pitted dates

$^1/_4$ cup dried fruit bits

Friends-of-the-Earth Vegan Muffins

It seemed that every time I brought my muffins into Friends of the Earth natural foods store where I sold them, the owners, Boyce and Tom, asked, "When are you gonna make us a vegan muffin?" Up to the task, I simply substituted cornstarch for eggs, left out the dairy, and included the great taste of walnuts, dates, and bananas. Talk about successful! You can create vegan muffins by substituting two tablespoons of cornstarch for the egg or egg whites, and soy milk for the cow's milk in any of my recipes.

1. Preheat the oven to 400°F.

2. Sift the dry ingredients together in a large bowl.

3. Whisk the wet ingredients in a medium bowl or blend in a food processor. Add the goodies and toss to coat. If necessary, use your hands to coat the gooey bits.

4. Pour the wet mixture into the dry ingredients. Stir just until mixed. *Do not overstir.*

5. Spoon the batter into a greased or papered muffin tin. Fill each cup nearly to the top.

6. Bake for 15 to 20 minutes.

7. Cool the muffins at least 10 minutes before removing from the tin.

Ladda's Lemon Ginger Muffins

Ladda is a Thai woman I met at a Buddhist monastery in England. Every Sunday, she'd arrive before mealtime and brew a huge pot of lemon ginger tea. It would simmer for about an hour while everyone waited in patient Buddhist style. We drank the tea all afternoon while learning about the Buddhist teachings from the monks and nuns. I created these muffins as a tribute to Ladda and the warmth she shared.

1. Preheat the oven to 375°F.

2. Sift the dry ingredients together in a large bowl.

3. Whisk the wet ingredients in a medium bowl or blend in a food processor. Add the goodies and stir to combine.

4. Pour the wet mixture into the dry ingredients. Stir just until mixed. *Do not overstir.*

5. Spoon the batter into a greased or papered muffin tin. Fill each cup nearly to the top.

6. Bake for 15 to 20 minutes.

7. Cool the muffins at least 10 minutes before removing from the tin.

YIELD 10–12 MUFFINS

DRY INGREDIENTS

1 1/2 cups whole wheat flour

1 1/2 cups unbleached white flour

2 tablespoons soy flour

2 teaspoons baking powder

1 teaspoon baking soda

1/4 teaspoon sea salt

1/2 teaspoon ground coriander

WET INGREDIENTS

1 3/4 cups milk

1/2 cup honey

1/4 cup canola oil

1 large egg

GOODIES

3 1/2 tablespoons grated lemon peel

3 tablespoons finely chopped fresh ginger root, or 1 1/2 tablespoons ground

YIELD
12
MUFFINS

DRY INGREDIENTS

1 cup whole wheat flour

3/4 cup barley flour

1/2 cup unbleached white flour

1/2 cup malted milk powder

1 1/2 teaspoons baking powder

1 teaspoon baking soda

1/4 teaspoon sea salt

WET INGREDIENTS

1 cup maple syrup

3/4 cup buttermilk

1/4 cup canola oil

1 large egg

GOODIES

1 1/4 cups chopped roasted pecans

Maple Pecan Muffins

On Saturday mornings, I like to go out for breakfast with my friends Donna and Cashin. We go to this very small, unassuming restaurant where every- thing is served up hot and homestyle. I never need to look at the menu because I know exactly what I want—pecan waffles with maple syrup. The waffles have a flavor unlike any others, which I discovered came from malt powder in the batter. My Maple Pecan Muffins bring forth that same wonderful flavor.

1. Preheat the oven to 400°F.

2. Sift the dry ingredients together in a large bowl.

3. Whisk the wet ingredients in a medium bowl or blend in a food processor. Add the goodies and stir to combine.

4. Pour the wet ingredients into the dry mixture. Stir just until mixed. *Do not overstir.*

5. Spoon the batter into a greased or papered muffin tin. Fill each cup nearly to the top.

6. Bake for 15 to 20 minutes.

7. Cool the muffins at least 10 minutes before removing from the tin.

Only-Kids-Need-Apply Muffins

If you love peanut butter, you're gonna love these muffins. You can make them with either chocolate chips or carob chips. Carob is a naturally sweet food that is similar to chocolate in flavor, but with less fat and about half the calories. It's also caffeine free. Is carob a substitute for chocolate? Not really, and it's probably best not to think of carob in that way. It has a flavor all its own. If you have a dairy allergy, be aware that most carob chips are not dairy free.

1. Preheat the oven to 400°F.

2. Sift the dry ingredients together in a large bowl. Add the chocolate chips and toss to coat.

3. Whisk the wet ingredients in a medium bowl or blend in a food processor. Pour the wet ingredients into the dry mixture. Stir just until mixed. *Do not overstir.*

4. Spoon the batter into a greased or papered muffin tin. Fill each cup nearly to the top.

5. Bake for 15 to 20 minutes.

6. Cool the muffins at least 10 minutes before removing from the tin.

YIELD
12 MUFFINS

DRY INGREDIENTS
I cup whole wheat pastry flour

I cup whole wheat flour

$\frac{1}{2}$ cup unbleached white flour

$\frac{1}{4}$ cup toasted wheat germ

2 teaspoons baking powder

I teaspoon baking soda

WET INGREDIENTS
I cup warm water

I cup milk

$\frac{1}{2}$ cup chunky peanut butter

$\frac{1}{4}$ cup canola oil

$\frac{1}{4}$ cup honey

I large egg

GOODIES
I $\frac{1}{4}$ cups semi-sweet chocolate or carob chips

Peanut Butter-Rice Cake Muffins

YIELD
12
MUFFINS

DRY INGREDIENTS

1 cup whole wheat pastry flour

$\frac{1}{2}$ cup whole wheat flour

$\frac{1}{2}$ cup unbleached white flour

$\frac{1}{2}$ cup brown rice flour

1 $\frac{1}{2}$ teaspoons baking powder

1 teaspoon baking soda

$\frac{3}{4}$ teaspoon ground cinnamon

$\frac{1}{4}$ teaspoon sea salt

WET INGREDIENTS

3 ripe bananas, mashed (1 $\frac{1}{2}$ cups)

$\frac{3}{4}$ cup milk

$\frac{1}{2}$ cup chunky peanut butter

$\frac{1}{2}$ cup rice syrup

$\frac{1}{4}$ cup canola oil

1 large egg

GOODIES

1 cup raisins

1 cup roasted sunflower seeds

Rice cakes are a rather benign, uninteresting food—pockets of air with the occasional vein of puffed rice. It wasn't until someone introduced me to rice cakes smothered with peanut butter, sliced bananas, raisins, roasted sunflower seeds, a drizzle of honey, and a sprinkle of cinnamon that I truly learned to appreciate rice cakes—probably because I couldn't taste them; I could only hear them crunch. Instead of using rice syrup in these muffins, you can use $\frac{1}{4}$ cup honey plus $\frac{1}{4}$ cup milk.

1. Preheat the oven to 375°F.

2. Sift the dry ingredients together in a large bowl.

3. Whisk the wet ingredients in a medium bowl. Add the goodies and stir to combine.

4. Pour the wet mixture into the dry ingredients. Stir just until mixed. *Do not overstir.*

5. Spoon the batter into a greased or papered muffin tin. Fill each cup nearly to the top.

6. Bake for 15 to 20 minutes.

7. Cool the muffins at least 10 minutes before removing from the tin.

Proof-of-the-Pudding Muffins

YIELD
12
MUFFINS

What is it about Indian pudding that makes me so happy? Ginger knocks me out, it's true. And not enough good things can be said about cinnamon. But there is something very earthy about the combination of cornmeal, milk, eggs, and molasses. Cervantes said, "The proof of the pudding is in the eating." Never was this more true than with Indian pudding.

1. Preheat the oven to 400°F.

2. Sift the dry ingredients together in a large bowl.

3. Whisk the wet ingredients together in a medium bowl or blend in a food processor. Add the goodies to the wet ingredients and stir to combine.

4. Pour the wet mixture into the dry ingredients. Stir just until mixed. *Do not overstir.*

5. Spoon the batter into a greased or papered muffin tin. Fill each cup nearly to the top.

6. Bake for 15 to 20 minutes.

7. Cool the muffins at least 10 minutes before removing from the tin.

DRY INGREDIENTS

- 2 cups whole wheat pastry flour
- 1 cup yellow cornmeal
- 2 teaspoons baking powder
- 1 teaspoon baking soda
- 1 teaspoon ground cinnamon
- $1/2$ teaspoon ground nutmeg
- $1/4$ teaspoon sea salt

WET INGREDIENTS

- $1\,3/4$ cups milk
- $1/4$ cup margarine or butter, melted
- $1/4$ cup molasses
- 1 large egg
- $1/2$ teaspoon vanilla extract

GOODIES

- $3/4$ cup raisins
- 2 tablespoons finely chopped fresh ginger root, or 1 tablespoon ground
- 2 teaspoons grated orange peel

YIELD
12
MUFFINS

Raspberry Bouquet Muffins

When it comes to berries, raspberries are the upper crust. They exude their "specialness" into everything they touch. My Raspberry Bouquet Muffins are no exception.

DRY INGREDIENTS

2 cups whole wheat pastry flour

$1/2$ cup unbleached white flour

2 teaspoons baking powder

I teaspoon baking soda

$1/4$ teaspoon sea salt

WET INGREDIENTS

I cup buttermilk

$1/2$ cup apple juice concentrate

$1/4$ cup canola oil

I large egg

I cup all-fruit raspberry jam

2 teaspoons grated lemon peel

$1 1/2$ teaspoons vanilla extract

$1 1/2$ teaspoons raspberry flavoring

GOODIES

$1 1/4$ cups firm fresh raspberries, washed, patted dry, and halved

1. Preheat the oven to 375°F.

2. Sift the dry ingredients together in a large bowl. Add the raspberries and toss to coat. (This will keep them from bleeding into the rest of the muffin.)

3. Whisk the wet ingredients in a medium bowl or blend in a food processor. Pour the wet ingredients into the dry mixture. Stir just until mixed, taking care not to break the raspberries. *Do not overstir.*

4. Spoon the batter into a greased or papered muffin tin. Fill each cup nearly to the top.

5. Bake for 15 to 20 minutes.

6. Cool the muffins at least 15 to 20 minutes before removing from the tin.

Working with Raspberries and Blackberries

When adding raspberries or blackberries to muffins, remember that they tend to lack the firmness of other berries, and can go all to pieces when baked. Take care to select the firmest fresh berries you can find. When they are not in season, use the frozen variety. After thawing, just be sure to drain them very well before adding to the dry ingredients. If the recipe also calls for apple juice concentrate, you can substitute up to $^1/_2$ cup of the concentrate with the drained raspberry or blackberry liquid. Just be aware that your muffins will be either red or blue if you make this substitution—but they will be just as delicious!

Soysage Cheese Muffins

YIELD
10–12
MUFFINS

DRY INGREDIENTS

1 ½ cup unbleached white flour

1 cup whole wheat flour

1 ½ teaspoon baking powder

1 teaspoon baking soda

1 teaspoon rubbed sage

¼ teaspoon sea salt

¼ teaspoon cayenne pepper

⅛ teaspoon black pepper

WET INGREDIENTS

1 cup buttermilk

¾ cup milk

¼ cup canola oil

1 large egg

GOODIES

¼ pound hot spicy soysage, crumbled

1 tablespoon canola oil

1 cup grated extra-sharp cheddar cheese

Sausage cheese balls—little biscuit-like puffs of bleached white flour made with hot pork sausage and cheddar cheese—are popular party hors d'oeuvres in the South. I decided to recreate a muffin with the flavor of these appealing appetizers by using soysage (a soybean product that tastes like sausage) and extra-sharp cheddar cheese. Soysage fries up nicely and resembles ground beef in texture and appearance. For this recipe, you'll want to end up with about 1 cup of browned ground soysage.

1. Preheat the oven to 400°F.

2. Place a medium skillet over medium heat. Add the soysage and tablespoon of canola oil, and sauté until the soysage is lightly browned. Transfer to paper towels and let drain.

3. Sift the dry ingredients together in a large bowl. Add the soysage and cheddar cheese and toss to coat. If necessary, crumble any large chunks of soysage.

4. Whisk the wet ingredients in a medium bowl or blend in a food processor. Pour the wet ingredients into the dry mixture. Stir just until mixed. *Do not overstir.*

5. Spoon the batter into a greased or papered muffin tin. Fill each cup nearly to the top.

6. Bake for 15 to 20 minutes.

7. Cool the muffins at least 10 minutes before removing from the tin.

Start-a-Movement Muffins

YIELD
12
MUFFINS

You say you're so backed up that every time you bend over you burp? You've tried everything from salt water to bran cakes and you're still about to bust? Is that what's bothering you, friend? Well, step right up and discover the power of prunes and bran—together for the first time in Start-a-Movement Muffins. If these don't do the job, nothing will. But don't eat more than one. Three prunes contain more fiber than a bowl of bran flakes, and these muffins have both! Try them with Sweet and Fruity Spread (page 191).

1. Preheat the oven to 400°F.

2. Sift together all the dry ingredients, except the bran, in a large bowl. Add the bran and stir to combine. Add the prunes and toss to coat. If necessary, use your hands to coat the gooey prune bits.

3. Whisk the wet ingredients in a medium bowl or blend in a food processor. Pour the wet ingredients into the dry mixture. Stir just until mixed. *Do not overstir.*

4. Spoon the batter into a greased or papered muffin tin. Fill each cup nearly to the top.

5. Bake for 15 to 20 minutes.

6. Cool the muffins at least 10 minutes before removing from the tin.

DRY INGREDIENTS

1 1/4 cups whole wheat flour

1 cup unbleached white flour

2 teaspoons baking powder

1 teaspoon baking soda

1 teaspoon ground cinnamon

1/4 teaspoon sea salt

1/2 cup wheat bran

WET INGREDIENTS

1 1/4 cups milk

1/2 cup apple juice concentrate

1/4 cup canola oil

1/4 cup molasses

1 large egg

2 teaspoons grated orange peel

GOODIES

1 1/2 cups chopped pitted prunes (about 24)

Thanks-to-the-Tropical-Sun Muffins

**YIELD
12
MUFFINS**

DRY INGREDIENTS

1 cup whole wheat pastry flour

1 cup unbleached white flour

3/4 cup whole wheat flour

2 teaspoons baking powder

1 teaspoon baking soda

1/4 teaspoon sea salt

WET INGREDIENTS

3/4 cup milk

1/2 cup peach or apricot all-fruit jam

1/4 cup canola oil

1 large egg

1 teaspoon rum extract

1 teaspoon grated lemon peel

GOODIES

16-ounce can mango, well drained (or enough fresh to yield 1 cup purée)

1 cup chopped dried papaya

These muffins are remisincent of a fresh fruit breakfast I had at a lovely little waterfront restaurant in Veracruz, Mexico. The platter was filled with sliced mango, papaya, and other tropical delights! Enough to feed four people! And, I might add, it was the most memorable serving of fruit I have ever eaten. Here's to that restaurant—whatever its name—and here's to the tropical sun that makes such wonderful fruits possible.

1. Preheat the oven to 375°F.

2. Sift the dry ingredients together in a large bowl. Add the papaya and toss to coat.

3. Purée the mangoes in a food processor or blender to yield about 1 cup. Add the wet ingredients and pulse to blend. (You can also use a fork or potato ricer to mash the mangoes, then blend the wet ingredients by hand.)

4. Pour the wet mixture into the dry mixture. Stir just until mixed. *Do not overstir.*

5. Spoon the batter into a greased or papered muffin tin. Fill each cup nearly to the top.

6. Bake for 15 to 20 minutes.

7. Cool the muffins at least 10 minutes before removing from the tin.

Very Berry Bran Muffins

What's a muffin cookbook without a berry muffin recipe? And what's a berry muffin without bran? Mmm. Mmm. As much as I love my other breakfast muffins, I have to admit that I make these most frequently. I think fresh blueberries and raspberries work best with this recipe. For an added treat, top them with Lemony Lemon Spread (page 190).

1. Preheat the oven to 375°F.

2. Sift all the dry ingredients, except the wheat bran, together in a large bowl. Then add the bran and stir to combine. Add the berries and toss to coat.

3. Whisk the wet ingredients in a medium bowl or blend in a food processor. Pour the wet ingredients into the dry mixture. Stir just until mixed. *Do not overstir.*

4. Spoon the batter into a greased or papered muffin tin. Fill each cup nearly to the top.

5. Bake for 15 to 20 minutes.

6. Cool the muffins at least 15 to 20 minutes before removing from the tin.

YIELD
12
MUFFINS

DRY INGREDIENTS
1 1/4 cups whole wheat pastry flour

1 1/4 cups whole wheat flour

1/2 cup light brown sugar

2 teaspoons baking powder

1 teaspoon baking soda

1/4 teaspoon sea salt

3/4 teaspoon ground cinnamon

3/4 teaspoon ground nutmeg

1 cup wheat bran

WET INGREDIENTS
1 1/2 cup buttermilk

1/4 cup canola oil

1/2 cup honey

1 large egg

1 teaspoon vanilla extract

1 teaspoon grated lemon peel

GOODIES
1 1/4 cups firm fresh berries, washed, patted dry, and chopped

3. **Crunchy,** Crumbly, Fruity, **Spicy** Do-Da **Muffins**

For those who like this sort of thing,
this is the sort of thing they like.

—SIR MAX BEERBOHM, SATIRIST AND AUTHOR

The idea for the muffin selection in this chapter grew out of a simple observation. I've noticed that whenever I enter a room with a basketful of muffins—whether to sell them at Friends of the Earth or to offer them at a party or potluck meal—people automatically reach for the ones with interesting crunchy or crumbly toppings.

"Ooo! What's that one?"

"Save me one with the stuff on top."

Granted, they are also interested in knowing whether any of the muffins in my basket contain chocolate. But that's another story and why I've included so many chocolate muffins in this book!

The topping doesn't have to be anything particularly complicated. A pinch of nuts or seeds, a sprinkling of toasted wheat germ, or a shred of coconut will do. The point is, more often than not, the crunchy crumbly muffins are the first ones to go.

This is an interesting phenomenon, and one that I fully understand. When ordering a meal in a restaurant or flipping through my cookbooks, I find I am usually drawn to the entrées that are smothered in a sauce or perhaps topped with a sprinkling of cheese. Given the option, I pick crumb cake over pound cake every time. And muffins with appealing crunchy crumbly toppings are hard to resist. I think we like having a little something extra to make what we eat feel special. And why not? It makes us giggle.

The only thing that can draw my attention away from the lure of crumbly toppings is spice. Spices tingle my taste buds. In fact, if you ask me which muffins are my favorites I'd say that I especially like the ones with lots of spice.

So here's a chapter with everybody's favorites—Crunchy, Crumbly, Fruity, Spicy Do-Da Muffins. What a mouthful! And are they ever!

Almond Delight Muffins

Place an almond between your back teeth and bite down a few times until you sense the almond flavor. Roll your tongue around the broken bits and let your taste buds do their thing. It's amazing. When the flavor bursts forth in my mouth, I feel a warm, almost numbing sensation in my throat. I notice that suddenly I'm more relaxed and I breathe more deeply, as if I am soaking in a bath of warm milk. Warm and soothing—that's what I should have called these muffins.

1. Preheat the oven to 400°F.

2. Sift the dry ingredients together in a large bowl.

3. Combine the goodies in a separate bowl. Reserve $^{1}/_{2}$ cup of this goodie mixture to top the muffins (see Step 5). Add the remaining mixture to the dry ingredients and stir to combine.

4. Whisk the wet ingredients in a medium bowl or blend in a food processor. Pour the wet ingredients into the dry mixture. Stir just until mixed. *Do not overstir.*

5. Spoon the batter into a greased or papered muffin tin. Fill each cup nearly to the top. Top each cup of batter with the remaining brown sugar and almond mixture, taking care to spread it evenly over each cup. Too much topping piled high in the middle will prevent the muffins from rising properly.

6. Bake for 15 to 20 minutes.

7. Cool the muffins at least 10 minutes before removing from the tin.

DRY INGREDIENTS

1 $^{1}/_{4}$ cups whole wheat pastry flour

1 cup whole wheat flour

$^{1}/_{2}$ cup unbleached white flour

1 $^{1}/_{2}$ teaspoons baking powder

$^{1}/_{4}$ teaspoon sea salt

$^{1}/_{2}$ teaspoon ground ginger

$^{1}/_{2}$ teaspoon ground cinnamon

$^{1}/_{2}$ teaspoon ground nutmeg

WET INGREDIENTS

1 $^{1}/_{2}$ cups milk

$^{3}/_{4}$ cup sour cream

1 large egg

1 $^{1}/_{2}$ teaspoons almond extract

1 teaspoon vanilla extract

GOODIES

1 cup coarsely chopped roasted almonds

$^{3}/_{4}$ cup dark brown sugar

Apple-Walnut Crumble Muffins

YIELD
12
MUFFINS

DRY INGREDIENTS

1 cup whole wheat flour

1 cup unbleached white flour

1 teaspoon baking powder

1 teaspoon baking soda

1 teaspoon ground cinnamon

$1/2$ teaspoon ground ginger

$1/4$ teaspoon sea salt

WET INGREDIENTS

1 $1/4$ cups buttermilk

$3/4$ cup applesauce

$1/2$ cup honey

1 large egg

1 teaspoon vanilla extract

GOODIES

1 medium apple, peeled
and chopped

1 cup chopped roasted
walnuts

CRUMBLE TOPPING

$1/2$ unbleached white flour

$1/4$ cup light brown sugar

$1/2$ teaspoon ground cinnamon

1 tablespoon margarine,
softened

I held a Sunday breakfast in honor of my nephew Rick's graduation from North Carolina School of the Arts. I could have served tea and toast as everyone's attention was clearly on Rick, but instead, I served these muffins with fresh fruit and coffee. In the years to come, we may forget exactly which muffins were served that day, but we will never forget the good feelings that they helped create. That's what great food does.

1. Preheat the oven to 400°F.

2. To prepare the crumble topping, combine the flour, brown sugar, and cinnamon in a medium bowl. Using a pastry blender or two knives, cut the margarine into the mixture to form crumbles. Set aside.

3. Sift the dry ingredients together in a large bowl. Add the goodies and toss to coat.

4. Whisk the wet ingredients in a medium bowl or blend in a food processor. Pour the wet ingredients into the dry mixture. Stir just until mixed. *Do not overstir.*

5. Spoon the batter into a greased or papered muffin tin. Fill each cup nearly to the top. Top each cup of batter with the crumble topping, taking care to spread it evenly over each cup. Too much topping piled high in the middle will prevent the muffins from rising properly.

6. Cool the muffins at least 10 minutes before removing from the tin.

Apple-iscious Apple Spice Muffins

YIELD
12
MUFFINS

The name for these muffins is pretty darn close to the sensation you'll experience while enjoying them. Say it and sense it—these muffins are apple-iscious! I think they are plenty sweet without the added sugar, but one of my testers feels they need more. I suggest trying them first without the sugar. If you feel they aren't sweet enough, add sugar the next time you make them. Try them with Peanut Butter and Apple Butter Spread (page 189).

1. Preheat the oven to 375°F.

2. To prepare the crunchy topping, combine the wheat germ and brown sugar in a small bowl and set aside.

3. Sift the dry ingredients together in a large bowl. Add the apples and toss to coat.

4. Whisk the wet ingredients in a medium bowl or blend in a food processor. Pour the wet ingredients into the dry mixture. Stir just until mixed. *Do not overstir.*

5. Spoon the batter into a greased or papered muffin tin. Fill each cup nearly to the top. Generously top each cup of batter with the crunchy topping, taking care to spread it evenly over each cup. Too much topping piled high in the middle will prevent the muffins from rising properly.

6. Bake for 15 to 20 minutes.

7. Cool the muffins at least 10 minutes before removing from the tin.

DRY INGREDIENTS

1 cup whole wheat pastry flour

1 cup whole wheat flour

1/2 cup barley flour

1/4 cup light brown sugar

1 1/2 teaspoons baking soda

1 teaspoon baking powder

1/4 teaspoon sea salt

1/4 teaspoon ground nutmeg

WET INGREDIENTS

1 1/2 cups milk

1 cup applesauce

1/4 cup apple butter

1 large egg

2 teaspoons grated lemon peel

1 teaspoon vanilla extract

GOODIES

2 medium apples, peeled and chopped

CRUNCHY TOPPING

1/2 cup honey crunch wheat germ

1/4 cup light brown sugar

Apricot-Sesame Muffins

**YIELD
12
MUFFINS**

DRY INGREDIENTS

I cup unbleached white flour

$^3/_4$ cup whole wheat pastry flour

$^1/_2$ cup brown rice flour

$^1/_2$ cup light brown sugar

I teaspoon baking powder

I teaspoon baking soda

$^1/_4$ teaspoon sea salt

WET INGREDIENTS

I cup buttermilk

I large egg

I teaspoon vanilla extract

GOODIES

I cup chopped dried apricots

16-ounce can apricots packed in fruit juice, well drained

TOPPING

3 tablespoons sesame seeds

I never liked apricots. When I was a kid, my family received a gift crate of dried fruits every Christmas. My sister Marlene always hogged the apricots, thinking they were great. Me? They made my lips pucker. I was in my mid-twenties before I even tried a fresh one, and was surprised to discover that it wasn't sour at all—at least when fresh. Drying seems to sharpen the flavor of apricots, make them tart. I created these muffins to blend the sweetness of apricots with their sharpness. It was a good idea.

1. Preheat the oven to 400°F.

2. Sift the dry ingredients together in a large bowl. Add the dried apricots and toss to coat.

3. Purée the canned apricots in a food processor or blender to yield about 1 cup purée. Add all of the wet ingredients and pulse to blend. (You can also use a fork or potato ricer to mash the apricots, and then blend in the wet ingredients by hand.)

4. Pour the wet mixture into the dry mixture. Stir just until mixed. *Do not overstir.*

5. Spoon the batter into a greased or papered muffin tin. Fill each cup nearly to the top. Top each cup of batter with a pinch of the sesame seeds, taking care to sprinkle them evenly over each cup.

6. Cool the muffins at least 10 minutes before removing from the tin.

Crazy About
Nuts and Seeds

Yep, the truth is that nuts and seeds have a relatively high fat content. With the exception of chestnuts, which contain less than 1 gram of fat per ounce and derive only 8 percent of their calories from fat, most nuts and seeds contain 15 to 20 grams of fat per ounce and derive more than 75 percent of their calories from fat. Does this mean you should avoid them? Absolutely not!

Fortunately, there are a number of other factors to consider. For one thing, it is important to understand that the fats contained in most nuts and seeds are almost entirely monounsaturated and polyunsaturated—the so-called "good" fats. They don't contain much saturated fat, which has been associated with heart disease, high cholesterol levels, and high blood pressure. In fact, unsaturated fats like the ones found in nuts and seeds have been shown to help *lower* these health risks. A study on macadamia nuts, for instance, indicated that they actually help lower blood pressure and reduce cholesterol. Other studies have shown that eating nuts may reduce the fatty substance that clogs arteries.

Besides, nuts and seeds contain important nutrients. They are an excellent source of protein, fiber, calcium, and magnesium. Some varieties supply vitamin E. And linoleic acid, a polyunsaturated fat found in nuts and seeds, is essential for life.

Does this mean we can gobble nuts and seeds by the handful? No. But it does mean that eating an ounce of nuts or seeds is not the same as eating an ounce of butter. We need certain fats in our diet, and nuts and seeds—basic and natural foods—are good sources of that fat.

Carrot Conglomeration Muffins

YIELD
12–14
MUFFINS

DRY INGREDIENTS

1 cup whole wheat pastry flour

$1/2$ cup whole wheat flour

$1/2$ cup unbleached white flour

$1/4$ cup light brown sugar

1 teaspoons baking powder

1 teaspoon baking soda

2 teaspoons ground cinnamon

$1/4$ teaspoon sea salt

WET INGREDIENTS

1 cup milk

$1/2$ cup apple juice concentrate

$1/4$ cup canola oil

1 large egg

2 tablespoons grated
orange peel

2 teaspoons vanilla extract

GOODIES

1 cup chopped apples

1 cup grated carrots

$1/2$ cup raisins or dried
pineapple

$1/2$ cup roasted sunflower
seeds

$1/2$ cup coconut

Sometimes I want to put everything but the kitchen sink into my muffins, especially when "everything" includes coconut, carrots, and apples. Kids love when I create mini-muffins from this recipe, so they can just pop them into their mouths. And for an alternative to the raisins, try dried pineapple (if you've ever had carrot cake with pineapple, you understand why). Apple Butter Spread (page 189) makes a great topping for these gems.

1. Preheat the oven to 400°F.

2. Sift the dry ingredients together in a large bowl. Add the goodies and toss to coat.

3. Whisk the wet ingredients in a medium bowl or blend in a food processor. Pour the wet ingredients into the dry mixture. Stir just until mixed. *Do not overstir.*

4. Spoon the batter into a greased or papered muffin tin. Fill each cup nearly to the top.

5. Bake for 15 to 20 minutes.

6. Cool the muffins at least 10 minutes before removing from the tin.

Chai Muffins

YIELD
12
MUFFINS

Chai is a popular drink in India and Sri Lanka and at Buddhist retreat centers and monasteries in the United States and Europe. I first enjoyed it when I took up meditation. Meditators bent on curbing their desire for sensory pleasure had a difficult time when the retreat staff served Chai. It is never a one-cup experience—only two or three will do. With my love for spicy cakes and breads, I realized that Chai's exotic blend of tea and spices would make a great muffin. See if you don't agree.

DRY INGREDIENTS

1 $^1/_4$ cups whole wheat flour

1 cup unbleached white flour

$^3/_4$ cup brown rice flour

$^1/_2$ cup light brown sugar

2 teaspoons baking powder

1 teaspoon baking soda

$^1/_4$ teaspoon sea salt

WET INGREDIENTS

$^1/_2$ cup honey

$^1/_4$ cup canola oil

1 large egg

GOODIES

1 $^3/_4$ cups water

2 tablespoons finely chopped fresh ginger root, or 1 tablespoon ground

$^1/_2$ teaspoon ground cinnamon

$^1/_4$ teaspoon ground anise

$^1/_4$ teaspoon ground cardamom

$^1/_4$ teaspoon ground cloves

2 black tea teabags

1. Combine all the goodie ingredients, except the tea, in a small saucepan and bring to a boil. Reduce the heat to medium-low and simmer for 30 minutes, or until the liquid reduces to 1$^1/_2$ cups. If necessary, add boiling water to get the right measure. Turn off the heat, add the tea, and steep for 10 minutes. Remove and discard the teabags, and allow the mixture to cool to room temperature.

2. Preheat the oven to 400°F.

3. Add the wet ingredients to the cooled tea mixture, and whisk to combine.

4. Sift the dry ingredients together in a large bowl. Pour the wet mixture into the dry ingredients. Stir just until mixed. *Do not overstir.*

5. Spoon the batter into a greased or papered muffin tin. Fill each cup nearly to the top.

6. Bake for 15 to 20 minutes.

7. Cool the muffins at least 10 minutes before removing from the tin.

**YIELD
12
MUFFINS**

Citrus-Poppy Seed Muffins

DRY INGREDIENTS

1 cup whole wheat flour

1 cup unbleached white flour

1 cup brown rice flour

$1/2$ cup light brown sugar

$1 1/2$ teaspoons baking powder

1 teaspoon baking soda

$1/4$ teaspoon sea salt

2 tablespoons poppy seeds

WET INGREDIENTS

1 cup milk

$3/4$ cup plain yogurt

$1/4$ cup honey

$1/4$ cup canola oil

1 large egg

3 tablespoons grated lemon or orange peel

1 teaspoon vanilla extract

The use of poppy seeds in baked goods is not a contemporary innovation. It goes back as far as ancient Greece and Asia. Maybe that's why most people enjoy them so much. By now, our pleasure is probably genetically determined. For an extra burst of poppy seed flavor, grind them with a mortar and pestle, whirl them in a food processor, or go high tech with an electric spice mill. Citrus Honey Glaze (page 192) is a great topper for these muffins.

1. Preheat the oven to 375°F.

2. Sift together all the dry ingredients, except the poppy seeds, in a large bowl. Add the poppy seeds and stir to combine.

3. Whisk the wet ingredients in a medium bowl or blend in a food processor. Pour the wet ingredients into the dry ingredients. Stir just until mixed. *Do not overstir.*

4. Spoon the batter into a greased or papered muffin tin. Fill each cup nearly to the top.

5. Bake for 15 to 20 minutes.

5. Cool the muffins at least 10 minutes before removing from the tin.

Cracked-Up Wheat Muffins

YIELD
12
MUFFINS

Cracked wheat isn't wheat that went crazy. It's raw whole wheat that was crushed up for you. Isn't that nice and convenient? It's also one of the most nutritious forms of wheat grain. To make this muffin quick and easy, I use bulgur—cracked wheat that has been cooked and dried. Bulgur needs just to be soaked in hot water to become a fluffy wheat delight. To make these muffins sweet, I use apple juice concentrate and dried apples. Try them warm from the oven with a slice of cheese. Mmm. Mmm.

1. Combine the goodies in a medium bowl, then let cool to room temperature.

2. Preheat the oven to 400°F.

3. Sift the dry ingredients together in a large bowl.

4. Whisk the wet ingredients in a medium bowl or blend in a food processor. Add the goodie mixture and stir to combine.

5. Pour the wet mixture into the dry ingredients. Stir just until mixed. *Do not overstir.*

6. Spoon the batter into a greased or papered muffin tin. Fill each cup nearly to the top.

7. Bake for 15 to 20 minutes.

8. Cool the muffins at least 10 minutes before removing from the tin.

DRY INGREDIENTS

2 cups whole wheat pastry flour

$1/2$ cup whole wheat flour

1 tablespoon baking powder

$1/4$ teaspoon sea salt

1 teaspoon ground cinnamon

WET INGREDIENTS

1 cup buttermilk

$1/2$ cup apple juice concentrate

$1/4$ cup margarine or butter, melted

1 large egg

GOODIES

$2 1/2$ cups boiling water

1 cup bulgur

$3/4$ cup chopped dried apples

YIELD
12
MUFFINS

DRY INGREDIENTS

1 1/2 cups whole wheat pastry flour

1 cup whole wheat flour

1 1/2 teaspoons baking powder

1 teaspoon baking soda

1 teaspoon ground cinnamon

1/4 teaspoon sea salt

WET INGREDIENTS

1 1/2 cups milk

1/4 cup canola oil

1/2 cup honey

1 tablespoon molasses

1 large egg

GOODIES

3/4 cup grated yellow squash and/or zucchini

3/4 cup chopped roasted walnuts

3/4 cup raisins

Dad's Summer Squash Muffins

In the summertime my dad used to grow tons of zucchini and squash. As you can imagine, by the middle of summer, my family was up to its ears in it. One year, I decided to create a squash muffin. Mmm. Mmm. As you'll see, mixing yellow squash and zucchini, half and half, results in colorful, delicious muffins that are great for dessert and breakfast, too. Enjoy them as you would zucchini bread—sliced, then topped with a little margarine, butter, or whipped cream cheese.

1. Preheat the oven to 400°F.

2. Sift the dry ingredients together in a large bowl. Add the goodies and toss to coat.

3. Whisk the wet ingredients in a medium bowl or blend in a food processor. Pour the wet ingredients into the dry mixture. Stir just until mixed. *Do not overstir.*

4. Spoon the batter into a greased or papered muffin tin. Fill each cup nearly to the top.

5. Bake for 15 to 20 minutes.

6. Cool the muffins at least 10 minutes before removing from the tin.

Far East Muffins

YIELD
10–12
MUFFINS

My nephew Ron is a martial artist, skilled in Kenpo Kosho Ryer—a Chinese form of karate that dates back to the thirteenth century. Here's a muffin for you, Ron. Made with a blend of spices from the part of the world that gave birth to Kenpo, these muffins are timeless. Enjoy them with Vanilla Cream Cheese Icing (page 193).

1. Preheat the oven to 400°F.

2. Sift the dry ingredients together in a large bowl.

3. Whisk the wet ingredients in a medium bowl or blend in a food processor. Pour the wet ingredients into the dry ingredients. Stir just until mixed. *Do not overstir.*

4. Spoon the batter into a greased or papered muffin tin. Fill each cup nearly to the top.

5. Cool the muffins at least 10 minutes before removing from the tin.

DRY INGREDIENTS

- 1 cup whole wheat pastry flour
- 1 cup brown rice flour
- 1/2 cup unbleached white flour
- 1 1/2 teaspoons baking soda
- 1 teaspoon baking powder
- 1 tablespoon ground ginger
- 1/2 teaspoon ground cardamom
- 1/4 teaspoon ground cinnamon
- 1/8 teaspoon ground cloves
- 1/4 teaspoon sea salt

WET INGREDIENTS

- 1 cup vanilla yogurt
- 1/2 cup milk
- 1/2 cup honey
- 1 large egg
- 2 teaspoons grated lemon peel

YIELD
12
MUFFINS

Lemon Pecan Muffins

DRY INGREDIENTS

1 $\frac{1}{2}$ cups whole wheat flour

1 cup unbleached white flour

$\frac{1}{2}$ cup light brown sugar

1 tablespoon baking powder

$\frac{1}{4}$ teaspoon sea salt

WET INGREDIENTS

1 cup buttermilk

$\frac{1}{2}$ cup apple juice concentrate

$\frac{1}{4}$ cup canola oil

1 large egg

3 tablespoons grated lemon peel

○ GOODIES

1 $\frac{1}{2}$ cup coarsely chopped roasted pecans

When I visit my Mom, she asks if I have any special requests. "Make a lemon pecan cake," I plead. But since Mom's in Pennsylvania and I'm in North Carolina, I visit only twice each year, so I don't get this cake as often as I would like. I created these muffins so I could enjoy the scrumptious ingredient combination more often. Now, when I visit my friends, I ask if they have any special requests. "Make us your Lemon Pecan Muffins," they plead.

1. Preheat the oven to 400°F.

2. Sift the dry ingredients together in a large bowl. Reserve $\frac{1}{2}$ cup of the pecans to top the muffins (see Step 4). Add the remaining pecans to the dry ingredients and toss to coat.

3. Whisk the wet ingredients in a medium bowl or blend in a food processor. Pour the wet ingredients into the dry mixture. Stir just until mixed. *Do not overstir.*

4. Spoon the batter into a greased or papered muffin tin. Fill each cup nearly to the top. Top each cup of batter with the reserved chopped pecans, taking care to sprinkle them evenly over each cup. Too much topping piled high in the middle will prevent the muffins from rising properly.

5. Bake for 15 to 20 minutes.

6. Cool the muffins at least 10 minutes before removing from the tin.

Mango with Crystallized Ginger Muffins

YIELD
12
MUFFINS

Mangoes are my favorite fruit. Sorry bananas. Sorry peaches. Sorry blueberries. You are wonderful but, I am afraid, wholly and utterly forgotten the minute I bite into a mango. In addition to its stop-the-world flavor, the mango is a rich source of vitamins, particularly vitamin C. It is also packed with beta-carotene, potassium, and fiber, and contains only about 100 calories. I enjoy mangoes sliced with a sprinkling of freshly grated ginger root. It's what inspired these muffins. I hope you enjoy them!

1. Preheat the oven to 375°F.

2. Sift the dry ingredients together in a large bowl. Add the crystallized ginger and toss to coat.

3. Purée the mangoes in a food processor or blender to yield about 1 cup. Add the wet ingredients and pulse to blend. (You can also use a fork or potato ricer to mash the mangoes, and then blend in the wet ingredients by hand.)

4. Pour the wet mixture into the dry mixture. Stir just until mixed. *Do not overstir.*

5. Spoon the batter into a greased or papered muffin tin. Fill each cup nearly to the top.

6. Bake for 15 to 20 minutes.

7. Cool the muffins at least 10 minutes before removing from the tin.

DRY INGREDIENTS

1 1/2 cups whole wheat flour

1 1/2 cups unbleached white flour

1/4 cup light brown sugar

2 teaspoons baking soda

1 teaspoon baking powder

1/4 teaspoon sea salt

WET INGREDIENTS

1 cup milk

1/2 cup honey

1 large egg

1 teaspoon rum flavoring

1 teaspoon grated lemon peel

GOODIES

3 tablespoons coarsely chopped crystallized ginger

16-ounce can mango, well drained (or enough fresh mango to yield 1 cup purée)

YIELD
12
MUFFINS

DRY INGREDIENTS

1 1/2 cups whole wheat pastry flour

1/2 cup whole wheat flour

1/2 cup unbleached white flour

2 1/2 teaspoons baking powder

1/2 cup light brown sugar

1 teaspoon cocoa powder

1 teaspoon ground cinnamon

1/2 teaspoon ground allspice

1/2 teaspoon ground nutmeg

1/4 teaspoon sea salt

WET INGREDIENTS

1 cup chunky applesauce

1 1/4 cups milk

1 large egg

GOODIES

3/4 cup chopped roasted walnuts

3/4 cup raisins

3/4 cup chopped pitted dates

Mom's Applesauce Muffins

Similar to a rich, dark apple pound cake, Mom's bridge party applesauce cake is always a crowd pleaser. Try this muffin adaptation of her recipe, and you'll agree that it's in a class all its own. Maybe it's the touch of cocoa that sets it apart. Maybe it's the dates. I don't know. But I do know that you are going to love these muffins, which are among my most frequently requested. And, oh, to save yourself some time, buy the dates already chopped.

1. Preheat the oven to 375°F.

2. Sift the dry ingredients together in a large bowl.

3. Whisk the wet ingredients in a medium bowl or blend in a food processor. Add the goodies and toss to coat. If necessary, use your hands to coat the gooey bits.

4. Pour the wet mixture into the dry ingredients. Stir just until mixed. *Do not overstir.*

5. Spoon the batter into a greased or papered muffin tin. Fill each cup nearly to the top.

6. Bake for 15 to 20 minutes.

7. Cool the muffins at least 10 minutes before removing from the tin.

Orange Cardamom Muffins

YIELD
12
MUFFINS

Cardamom is that wonderful spice that gives coffeecakes and Danish pastries their distinctive flavor. It is native to India, but cultivated and used extensively throughout Southeast Asia in curries, cakes, and spiced teas. Cardamom is probably my favorite spice, and I expect these muffins will show you why. You can buy prepackaged slivered almonds for this recipe. It doesn't make sense to try to sliver them yourself. Try these muffins with Lemon Spread (page 190).

DRY INGREDIENTS

1 ½ cups whole wheat flour

1 ½ cups whole wheat pastry flour

¼ cup light brown sugar

2 teaspoons baking powder

1 teaspoon baking soda

1 ¼ teaspoons ground cardamom

¼ teaspoon sea salt

WET INGREDIENTS

1 ½ cup buttermilk

½ cup honey

¼ cup canola oil

1 large egg

3 tablespoons grated orange peel

TOPPING

¾ cup slivered almonds

1. Preheat the oven to 400°F.

2. Sift the dry ingredients together in a large bowl.

3. Whisk the wet ingredients in a medium bowl or blend in a food processor. Pour the wet ingredients into the dry ingredients. Stir just until mixed. *Do not overstir.*

4. Spoon the batter into a greased or papered muffin tin. Fill each cup nearly to the top. Top each cup of batter with a large pinch of slivered almonds, taking care to sprinkle them evenly over each cup. Too much topping piled high in the middle will prevent the muffins from rising properly.

5. Bake for 15 to 20 minutes.

6. Cool the muffins at least 10 minutes before removing from the tin.

Peachy Peach Muffins

DRY INGREDIENTS

1 cup whole wheat pastry flour

1 cup unbleached white flour

$^3/_4$ cup whole wheat flour

$^1/_4$ cup light brown sugar

2 teaspoons baking powder

1 teaspoon baking soda

$^1/_4$ teaspoon ground nutmeg

$^1/_4$ teaspoon sea salt

WET INGREDIENTS

1 cup milk

$^1/_2$ cup peach all-fruit jam

$^1/_4$ cup canola oil

1 large egg

1 teaspoon rum extract

1 teaspoon grated orange peel

GOODIES

1 cup chopped dried peaches

16-ounce can peaches packed in fruit juice, well drained

I love it when peaches, cantaloupe, and blueberries come into season together, don't you? Why try to improve on nature? I make these muffins with canned peaches (fresh are too acidic), and then serve them with fresh blueberries and cantaloupe.

1. Preheat the oven to 400°F.

2. Sift the dry ingredients together in a large bowl. Add the dried peaches and toss to coat.

3. Purée the canned peaches in a food processor or blender to yield about 1 cup. Add the wet ingredients and pulse to blend. (You can also use a fork or potato ricer to mash the peaches, and then blend in the wet ingredients by hand.)

4. Pour the wet mixture into the dry mixture. Stir just until mixed. *Do not overstir.*

5. Spoon the batter into a greased or papered muffin tin. Fill each cup nearly to the top.

6. Bake for 15 to 20 minutes.

7. Cool the muffins at least 10 minutes before removing from the tin.

Prune Spice Muffins

When I first made this recipe and tossed the prune bits in the dry ingredients, I noticed they remained clumped together. "Get your hands into it," came a fun-loving inner voice. Yeah. That's right. We don't have to be limited by our manufactured tools, do we? Sometimes our hands are the best tools we have. Get your hands in it. Use your fingers to coat the individual prune bits with flour. It's a very satisfying experience.

1. Preheat the oven to 400°F.

2. Sift together all the dry ingredients, except the bran, in a large bowl. Add the bran and stir to combine. Add the goodies and toss to coat. If necessary, use your hands to coat the gooey bits.

3. Whisk the wet ingredients in a medium bowl or blend in a food processor. Pour the wet ingredients into the dry mixture. Stir just until mixed. *Do not overstir.*

4. Spoon the batter into a greased or papered muffin tin. Fill each cup nearly to the top.

5. Bake for 15 to 20 minutes.

6. Cool the muffins at least 10 minutes before removing from the tin.

DRY INGREDIENTS

3/4 cup whole wheat flour

3/4 cup unbleached white flour

3/4 cup barley flour

1/2 cup light brown sugar

1 1/2 teaspoons baking powder

1 teaspoon baking soda

1 teaspoon ground cinnamon

1 teaspoon ground allspice

1/2 teaspoon ground cloves

1/4 teaspoon sea salt

2 tablespoons oat or wheat bran

WET INGREDIENTS

1 1/4 cups buttermilk

1/4 cup apple juice concentrate

1/4 cup canola oil

1 large egg

GOODIES

3/4 cup chopped pitted prunes (about 12)

1/2 cup chopped roasted walnuts

YIELD
12–14
MUFFINS

DRY INGREDIENTS

1 $\frac{1}{2}$ cup whole wheat flour

$\frac{1}{2}$ cup unbleached white flour

$\frac{1}{2}$ cup light brown sugar

2 teaspoons baking powder

$\frac{1}{2}$ teaspoon baking soda

$\frac{1}{2}$ teaspoon ground cinnamon

$\frac{1}{4}$ teaspoon sea salt

WET INGREDIENTS

2 cups buttermilk

$\frac{1}{4}$ cup canola oil

1 large egg

2 teaspoons vanilla extract

GOODIES

$\frac{1}{2}$ cup granola

$\frac{1}{2}$ cup semi-sweet chocolate or carob chips

$\frac{1}{2}$ cup flaked coconut

$\frac{1}{2}$ cup coarsely chopped roasted walnuts

$\frac{1}{2}$ cup roasted sunflower seeds

TOPPING

$\frac{1}{4}$ cup flaked coconut

Seven-Factors-of-Enlightenment Muffins

In Buddhism, there are seven factors or states of mind that are present in the heart and mind when we are seeing clearly. They are mindfulness, investigation, effort, rapture, concentration, tranquility, and equanimity. These Seven-Factors-of-Enlightenment Muffins include seven wonderful ingredients—applesauce, brown sugar, granola, chocolate or carob chips, flaked coconut, roasted walnuts, and roasted sunflower seeds. Try them and discover their enlightening qualities.

1. Preheat the oven to 375°F.

2. Sift the dry ingredients together in a large bowl. Add the goodies and toss to coat.

3. Whisk the wet ingredients in a medium bowl or blend in a food processor. Pour the wet ingredients into the dry mixture. Stir just until mixed. *Do not overstir.*

4. Spoon the batter into a greased or papered muffin tin. Fill each cup nearly to the top. Top each cup of batter with a pinch of coconut, taking care to sprinkle it evenly over each cup. Too much topping piled high in the middle will prevent the muffins from rising properly.

5. Bake for 15 to 20 minutes.

6. Cool the muffins at least 10 minutes before removing from the tin.

Spice Muffins with Vanilla Cream Cheese Icing

When I first started cooking, I was perfectly satisfied with a twelve-bottle spice rack. A few years later, I replaced it with an eighteen-bottle set. Before long, I found myself coveting my friend Deb's twenty-bottle rack that spun on the countertop, and Maury and Grethe's wall cabinet that opened into a multileveled spice junkie's dream. I cannot imagine life without spices. I use them in everything—in tea, on toast, in ethnic-style dishes, and certainly in muffins.

1. Preheat the oven to 375°F.

2. Sift the dry ingredients together in a large bowl.

3. Whisk the wet ingredients in a medium bowl or blend in a food processor. Add the goodies and stir to combine.

4. Pour the wet mixture into the dry ingredients. Stir just until mixed. *Do not overstir.*

5. Spoon the batter into a greased or papered muffin tin. Fill each cup nearly to the top.

6. Bake for 15 to 20 minutes.

7. Cool the muffins at least 10 minutes before removing from the tin. Allow them to further cool to room temperature before adding the icing.

DRY INGREDIENTS

1 $\frac{1}{4}$ cups whole wheat pastry flour

1 cup whole wheat flour

$\frac{1}{2}$ cup dark brown sugar

1 teaspoon baking powder

1 teaspoon baking soda

1 teaspoon ground cinnamon

$\frac{1}{2}$ teaspoon ground nutmeg

$\frac{1}{2}$ teaspoon ground ginger

$\frac{1}{4}$ teaspoon sea salt

WET INGREDIENTS

1 $\frac{1}{4}$ cups buttermilk

1 cup applesauce

$\frac{1}{4}$ cup honey

1 large egg

2 teaspoons grated orange peel

1 teaspoon vanilla extract

GOODIES

$\frac{3}{4}$ cup golden raisins

TOPPING

Vanilla Cream Cheese Icing (page 193)

YIELD
12
MUFFINS

DRY INGREDIENTS

I cup unbleached white flour

$1/2$ cup whole wheat flour

$1/2$ cup brown rice flour

$1/2$ cup light brown sugar

I teaspoon baking powder

I teaspoon baking soda

$1/4$ teaspoon sea salt

WET INGREDIENTS

I $1/4$ cups milk

$1/4$ cup canola oil

I large egg

2 teaspoons grated
orange peel

GOODIES

I cup dried apricots,
chopped

$1/2$ cup flaked coconut

16-ounce can apricots
packed in fruit juice,
well drained

TOPPING

$1/4$ cup all-fruit apricot
preserves

$1/2$ cup flaked coconut

Triple-Apricot Ambrosia Muffins

The checkout clerk looked at the name on my charge card. "Ambrosia. What a delicious name! I just love ambrosia salad, don't you?" I assured her that I did. "I make mine with oranges and coconut. How do you make yours?" she asked. I told her that I used to make it that way until I discovered how delicious it is with fresh apricots and just a hint of orange. My Triple Apricot Ambrosia Muffins match my ambrosia salad. They are rich in fruity and coconut-y flavor.

1. Preheat the oven to 375°F.

2. Sift the dry ingredients together in a large bowl. Add the dried apricots and coconut and toss to coat.

3. Purée the canned apricots in a food processor or blender to yield about 1 cup. Add the wet ingredients and pulse to blend. (You can also use a fork or potato ricer to mash the peaches, and then blend in the wet ingredients by hand.)

4. Pour the wet mixture into the dry mixture. Stir just until mixed. *Do not overstir.*

5. Spoon the batter into a greased or papered muffin tin. Fill each cup nearly to the top.

6. Bake for 15 to 20 minutes.

7. Cool the muffins at least 10 minutes before removing from the tin. When they have further cooled to room temperature, spread a teaspoon of apricot preserves on top of each and sprinkle with a large pinch of coconut.

Tropical Fruit Muffins

I scoured the marketplace for the best dried fruit to create a tropical fruit muffin. Unexpectedly, I discovered an outstanding product in my local grocery store. Packaged by Mariani Packing Company in San Jose, California, Premium Tropical Medley contains pineapple, apricots, papaya, dark raisins, golden raisins, apples, and even coconut. Yet the chopped fruit conglomeration contains only one gram of fat per ounce! In addition to being delicious, these high-carbohydrate, low-fat muffins are energizing.

1. Preheat the oven to 400°F.

2. Sift the dry ingredients together in a large bowl.

3. Whisk the wet ingredients in a medium bowl or blend in a food processor. Add the dried fruit and stir to combine.

4. Pour the wet mixture into the dry ingredients. Stir just until mixed. *Do not overstir.*

5. Spoon the batter into a greased or papered muffin tin. Fill each cup nearly to the top.

6. Bake for 15 to 20 minutes.

7. Cool the muffins at least 10 minutes before removing from the tin.

YIELD 12 MUFFINS

DRY INGREDIENTS

1 1/4 cups unbleached white flour

1 cup whole wheat flour

1/2 cup brown rice flour

1/4 cup light brown sugar

1 1/2 teaspoons baking soda

1 teaspoon baking powder

1/4 teaspoon sea salt

WET INGREDIENTS

1 1/2 cups milk

1 ripe banana, mashed (1/2 cup)

1/2 cup honey

1 large egg

2 teaspoons rum flavoring

1 tablespoon grated orange peel

GOODIES

1 cup dried tropical fruit mix

4. **Herby** Cheesy Muffin **Thangs**

For a man seldom thinks with more earnestness
of anything than he does his dinner.

—SAMUEL JOHNSON, WRITER

I like my life to be coordinated. When I wear a pink T-shirt, I want to wear pink socks, not yellow. When I eat Chinese food, I want a fortune cookie or almond cookie for dessert, not New York cheesecake. You know what I mean? That's why I wrote this chapter. With Herby Cheesy Muffin Thangs, you can bake muffins to match any cuisine—from simple dishes to gourmet fare—and provide a memorable accompaniment to your meal at the same time. In fact, with Herby Cheesy Muffin Thangs you can *create* the cuisine—Italian, French, Chinese, Japanese, Indian, Middle Eastern, Jewish, Mexican, and good old American. Just add a salad and a simple bowl of soup and, presto . . . an unforgettable meal.

When people think of muffins, I suspect that most imagine sweet treats made with fruits and nuts and such. This is probably because muffins are usually relegated exclusively to the breakfast table. This chapter is devoted to a new kind of muffin. For my Herby Cheesy Muffin Thangs, I have left out the sweeteners and added veggies, cheese, and/or herbs. You can enjoy these fabulous savory dinner muffins with soups, salads, casseroles, and every kind of meal imaginable. I had Italian meals in mind when I made my Mama Mia Muffins and Tomato Basil Muffins; Indian cuisine for my Chutney Muffins and Cashew Curry Muffins; and soups and salads for my Artichoke Hearts with Basil Muffins, French Onion Muffins, and Garden Vegetable Cream Cheese Muffins. You'll find that my Mexicali Corn Muffins and Hushpuppy Muffins go great with refried beans.

Herby Cheesy Muffin Thangs are a quick, easy, and welcome change from breads and dinner rolls. I am not putting ordinary bread down. I love it. But you have to admit that bread is often an unintegrated part of the meal. It may be served with the meal, but really isn't part of it. Even the most interesting bread seems to sit in the back row. Herby Cheesy Muffin Thangs, on the other hand, are so interesting that they can claim center stage.

I use vegetable broth in many of the muffins in this chapter to give them added flavor and nutrition. Make it easy on yourself by using powdered vegetable boullion. When mixed with water, it becomes wholesome broth without a lot of fuss and muss.

With Herby Cheesy Muffin Thangs, you can enjoy a muffin with a meal—or a meal with a muffin!

Roasted Red Pepper Muffins

YIELD
10–12
MUFFINS

When my sister Betty gave me a jar of roasted red peppers nestled in a basketful of interesting sauces and condiments, I immediately thought of using them in a muffin. But I didn't so much as sift the flour until I got a sign from heaven, indicating the perfect ingredients to go with the peppers. One afternoon, while in the cheese department of my local grocery store, I saw it—a container of cream cheese flavored with garlic and herbs. "Eureka." I knew it was the sign I'd been looking for.

DRY INGREDIENTS

1 cup whole wheat flour

1 cup unbleached white flour

$\frac{1}{2}$ cup brown rice flour

1 $\frac{1}{2}$ teaspoons baking powder

1 teaspoon baking soda

$\frac{1}{4}$ teaspoon sea salt

WET INGREDIENTS

6 ounces garlic and herb cream cheese, softened

1 $\frac{1}{4}$ cups milk

1 tablespoon olive oil

1 large egg

GOODIES

$\frac{1}{2}$ cup chopped roasted red peppers

2 teaspoons fresh rosemary, or 1 teaspoon dried

1. Preheat the oven to 400°F.

2. Sift together all the dry ingredients in a large bowl.

3. Whisk the wet ingredients in a medium bowl or blend in a food processor. Add the goodies and stir to combine.

4. Pour the wet ingredients into the dry mixture. Stir just until mixed. *Do not overstir.*

5. Spoon the batter into a greased or papered muffin tin. Fill each cup nearly to the top.

6. Bake for 15 to 20 minutes.

7. Cool the muffins at least 10 minutes before removing from the tin.

YIELD
12
MUFFINS

DRY INGREDIENTS

1 cup whole wheat pastry flour

$\frac{1}{2}$ cup whole wheat flour

$\frac{1}{2}$ cup unbleached white flour

$2\frac{1}{2}$ teaspoons baking powder

$\frac{1}{4}$ teaspoon sea salt

$\frac{1}{4}$ teaspoon ground black pepper

$\frac{1}{2}$ cup grated Parmesan cheese

WET INGREDIENTS

1 cup vegetable broth

$\frac{3}{4}$ cup milk

$\frac{1}{4}$ cup olive oil

1 large egg

GOODIES

4 canned artichoke hearts (water-packed), drained and chopped by hand

$\frac{1}{2}$ cup chopped fresh basil

1 clove garlic, minced

Artichoke Hearts with Basil Muffins

Remember your first artichoke? I can't forget it. I scraped and sucked every morsel of flesh from the succulent leaves—all the while noticing that the deeper into the artichoke I went, the sweeter it got. And just when I thought this delectable experience was drawing to a close, I discovered that the best of the artichoke was before me—the exquisite, tender heart. I asked myself, "Where have I been all my life?" I believe you will agree that I have done justice to this wonder with these muffins.

1. Preheat the oven to 400°F.

2. Sift together all the dry ingredients, except the Parmesan cheese, in a large bowl. Then add the cheese and stir to combine.

3. Whisk the wet ingredients in a medium bowl or blend in a food processor. Add the goodies and stir to combine.

4. Pour the wet mixture into the dry ingredients. Stir just until mixed. *Do not overstir.*

5. Spoon the batter into a greased or papered muffin tin. Fill each cup nearly to the top.

6. Bake for 15 to 20 minutes.

7. Cool the muffins at least 10 minutes before removing from the tin.

Barley-Mushroom Muffins

YIELD
10–12
MUFFINS

These muffins are good for the heart, easy on the purse, and delightful to the palate. The recipe calls for nutritional yeast flakes, which you can buy at your health food store. If you have never cooked with nutritional yeast flakes, you are in for a taste treat. My love affair with it began several years ago when I first used it in a gravy. It has one of those tastes I can't describe. You'll have to sample it for yourself. So try it, you'll like it!

1. To prepare the goodie mixture, bring the water to a boil. Add the barley, cover, and simmer for 20 minutes or until the barley is soft (it should measure 1 cup). Transfer the barley to a medium bowl and add the remaining goodie ingredients. Stir to combine, and set aside.

2. Preheat the oven to 400°F.

3. Sift together all the dry ingredients, except the nutritional yeast, in a large bowl. Then add the nutritional yeast and stir to combine.

4. Whisk the wet ingredients in a medium bowl or blend in a food processor. Add the wet ingredients to the goodie mixture and combine.

5. Pour the wet mixture into the dry ingredients. Stir just until mixed. *Do not overstir.*

6. Spoon the batter into a greased or papered muffin tin. Fill each cup nearly to the top.

7. Bake for 20 to 25 minutes.

8. Cool the muffins at least 10 minutes before removing from the tin.

DRY INGREDIENTS

1 cup whole wheat pastry flour

$\frac{1}{2}$ cup whole wheat flour

$\frac{1}{2}$ cup unbleached white flour

$\frac{1}{2}$ cup barley flour

1 tablespoon baking powder

$\frac{1}{4}$ teaspoon ground black pepper

2 tablespoons nutritional yeast flakes

WET INGREDIENTS

1 cup vegetable broth

$\frac{1}{2}$ cup milk

$\frac{1}{4}$ cup olive oil

$\frac{1}{4}$ cup soy sauce

1 large egg

GOODIES

$\frac{2}{3}$ cup water

$\frac{1}{3}$ cup whole grain barley

1 cup chopped mushrooms

2 tablespoons chopped onion

$\frac{1}{4}$ cup grated carrot

1 teaspoon dried basil

YIELD
10–12
MUFFINS

Béarnaise Muffins

DRY INGREDIENTS

2 ½ cups whole wheat pastry flour

½ cup unbleached white flour

2 teaspoons baking powder

½ teaspoon baking soda

¼ teaspoon ground pepper

WET INGREDIENTS

I cup vegetable broth

½ cup milk

¼ cup cooking sherry

¼ cup olive oil

I large egg

GOODIES

2 teaspoons chopped onion

I tablespoon soy sauce

2 teaspoons Dijon mustard

I ½ tablespoons dried tarragon

I tablespoon chopped chives

I teaspoon grated lemon peel

Béarnaise sauce is not among my most repeated recipes, yet every time I make it to spoon over asparagus or egg dishes, I exclaim, "This is wonderful! Why don't I make it more often?" In between servings, I miss béarnaise. The thought of it makes me smile with fond memories. I invented these muffins to bring this sauce back into my life—and yours. They go great with cream of asparagus soup or miso broth and a fresh garden salad.

1. Preheat the oven to 400°F.

2. Sift the dry ingredients together in a large bowl.

3. Whisk the wet ingredients in a medium bowl or blend in a food processor. Add the goodies and stir to combine.

4. Pour the wet mixture into the dry ingredients. Stir just until mixed. *Do not overstir.*

5. Spoon the batter into a greased or papered muffin tin. Fill each cup nearly to the top.

6. Bake for 15 to 20 minutes.

7. Cool the muffins at least 10 minutes before removing from the tin.

Brie-with-Brandy Muffins

My friend Steven's Brie-with-brandy spread has such a delicious combination of flavors that it was destined to inspire a muffin recipe. When served with sliced fruit and tea, my Brie-with-Brandy Muffins are part of an amazing meal. Because of the golden raisins and brown sugar, they are also sweet enough to serve for dessert (with sliced apples!).

DRY INGREDIENTS

2 cups whole wheat pastry flour

$^1/_2$ cup unbleached white flour

1 tablespoon baking powder

$^1/_2$ teaspoon baking soda

$^1/_4$ teaspoon sea salt

WET INGREDIENTS

8-ounces Brie cheese

1 $^1/_4$ cups milk

$^1/_4$ cup canola oil

1 large egg

2 teaspoons brandy extract

GOODIES

1 cup slivered almonds

1 cup golden raisins

$^1/_4$ cup light brown sugar

TOPPING

$^1/_2$ cup slivered almonds

1. Preheat the oven to 400°F.

2. Sift the dry ingredients together in a large bowl.

3. Place the Brie and milk in a saucepan over medium heat, and stir until the Brie is melted. Transfer to a medium bowl along with the remaining wet ingredients and whisk together. Add the goodies and stir to combine.

4. Pour the wet mixture into the dry ingredients. Stir just until mixed. *Do not overstir.*

5. Spoon the batter into a greased or papered muffin tin. Fill each cup nearly to the top.

6. Top each cup of batter with a large pinch of slivered almonds, taking care to sprinkle them evenly over each cup.

7. Bake for 15 to 20 minutes.

8. Cool the muffins at least 10 minutes before removing from the tin.

Cashew Curry Muffins

DRY INGREDIENTS

2 cups whole wheat pastry flour

$1/2$ cup unbleached white flour

2 teaspoons baking powder

$1/2$ teaspoon baking soda

2 tablespoons light brown sugar

2 tablespoons curry powder

$1/4$ teaspoon sea salt

WET INGREDIENTS

$1 1/4$ cups vegetable broth

$1/2$ cup milk

$1/4$ cup olive oil

I large egg

GOODIES

I cup coarsely chopped roasted cashews

$3/4$ cup chopped apples

$3/4$ cup raisins

$1/2$ cup flaked coconut

2 cloves minced garlic

I tablespoon finely chopped fresh ginger root, or
$1 1/2$ teaspoons ground

TOPPING

$1/2$ cup chopped roasted cashews

Ever since I began cooking, I've enjoyed eating curried "anything." But it wasn't until recently that I learned there are as many blends of curry powder as there are uses for it! And now I've added one more use— muffins! If you are familiar with various curry powders, choose the one that you like best for this recipe. Any blend will provide mouth-watering results. Try these muffins with stir-fry veggies, a garden salad, or a bowl of carrot or tomato soup.

1. Preheat the oven to 400°F.

2. Sift the dry ingredients together in a large bowl.

3. Whisk the wet ingredients in a medium bowl or blend in a food processor. Add the goodies and stir to combine.

4. Pour the wet mixture into the dry ingredients. Stir just until mixed. *Do not overstir.*

5. Spoon the batter into a greased or papered muffin tin. Fill each cup nearly to the top. Top each cup of batter with a large pinch of cashews, taking care to sprinkle them evenly over each cup.

6. Bake for 15 to 20 minutes.

7. Cool the muffins at least 10 minutes before removing from the tin.

Chutney Muffins

**YIELD
10
MUFFINS**

A delectable relish-y condiment made from fresh and dried fruits, sweetener, vinegar, and spices, chutney is commonly enjoyed with curried dishes. Be aware that each chutney type has its own distinct flavor, so you may want to try a few before choosing one for these muffins—or you can make your own. Just be aware that the chutney used in this recipe should have the texture of pickle relish. If it's too dry, add a little broth or water. If it's runny, reduce the amount of broth called for in this recipe.

DRY INGREDIENTS

2 cups whole wheat pastry flour

$1/2$ cup unbleached white flour

2 tablespoons soy flour

1 tablespoon baking powder

WET INGREDIENTS

1 cup vegetable broth

$1/4$ cup canola oil

1 large egg

GOODIES

1 $1/2$ cups coarsely chopped chutney

1. Preheat the oven to 400°F.

2. Sift the dry ingredients together in a large bowl.

3. Whisk the wet ingredients together in a medium bowl or blend in a food processor. Add the chutney and stir to combine.

4. Pour the wet mixture into the dry ingredients. Stir just until mixed. *Do not overstir.*

5. Spoon the batter into a greased or papered muffin tin. Fill each cup nearly to the top.

6. Bake for 15 to 20 minutes.

7. Cool the muffins at least 10 minutes before removing from the tin.

Cosmic Cottage Dill Muffins

**YIELD
12
MUFFINS**

DRY INGREDIENTS
1 ½ cups whole wheat flour

1 ½ cups unbleached white flour

1 tablespoon baking powder

¼ teaspoon sea salt

2 tablespoons wheat or oat bran

WET INGREDIENTS
1 ¼ cups milk

1 cup cottage cheese

¼ cup canola oil

1 large egg

1 tablespoon honey

GOODIES
2 tablespoons chopped onion

2 tablespoons dill seeds

Back in college, I made my sister Diane a loaf of cottage dill bread. Since then, she has asked for it nearly every time we get together. The bread naturally evolved into these muffins. Now when I visit Diane, I make her a couple dozen Cosmic Cottage Dill Muffins, so she and her family can eat one dozen and freeze the second (although the second dozen rarely makes it to the freezer). Great with any meal, these muffins go especially well with simple vegetable or egg dishes.

1. Preheat the oven to 400°F.

2. Sift together all the dry ingredients, except the bran, in a large bowl. Add the bran and stir to combine.

3. Whisk the wet ingredients in a medium bowl. Do not use a blender or food processor. Add the goodies and stir to combine.

4. Pour the wet mixture into the dry ingredients. Stir just until mixed. *Do not overstir.*

5. Spoon the batter into a greased or papered muffin tin. Fill each cup nearly to the top.

6. Bake for 15 to 20 minutes.

7. Cool the muffins at least 10 minutes before removing from the tin.

French Onion Muffins

YIELD
11–12
MUFFINS

I've always been fond of French onion soup. Whenever I see it on a menu, I order it. When I discovered the combination of toasted nutritional yeast flakes and soy sauce mimics the flavor of the consommé used in this classic soup, I immediately thought, "Why not a French onion muffin?" Although this recipe calls for regular Swiss cheese, you can also use Swiss cheese made with skim milk to create a low-fat version of these delicious gems.

1. To prepare the goodie mixture, heat the olive oil in a small skillet over medium heat. Add the onion, garlic, and tarragon, and cook until soft—about 5 minutes. Remove from the heat and let cool to room temperature.

2. Preheat the oven to 400°F.

3. Sift together all of the dry ingredients, except the nutritional yeast flakes, in a large bowl and set aside.

4. In a small skillet, toast the yeast flakes over medium heat until they begin to brown. Add them to the dry ingredients along with the Swiss cheese, and stir to combine.

5. Whisk the wet ingredients in a medium bowl or blend in a food processor. Add the goodie mixture and stir to combine.

6. Pour the wet mixture into the dry ingredients. Stir just until mixed. *Do not overstir.*

7. Spoon the batter into a greased or papered muffin tin. Fill each cup nearly to the top.

8. Cool the muffins at least 10 minutes before removing from the tin.

DRY INGREDIENTS

1 ½ cups whole wheat flour

1 cup unbleached white flour

1 ½ teaspoons baking powder

1 teaspoon baking soda

¼ teaspoon ground pepper

½ cup nutritional yeast flakes

WET INGREDIENTS

1 cup vegetable broth

¾ cup milk

1 large egg

1 tablespoon soy sauce

2 teaspoons Dijon mustard

2 teaspoons honey

GOODIES

3 ounces Swiss cheese, grated

2 tablespoons olive oil

3 tablespoons chopped onion

2 cloves garlic, minced

1 ½ tablespoons dried tarragon

Garden Vegetable Cream Cheese Muffins

DRY INGREDIENTS

1 1/2 cups whole wheat flour

1 1/4 cups unbleached white flour

1 1/2 teaspoons baking powder

1 1/2 teaspoons baking soda

1/4 teaspoon sea salt

2 tablespoons light brown sugar

1/4 cup oat bran

1/2 teaspoon basil leaves

1/2 teaspoon rubbed sage

1/4 teaspoon ground thyme

WET INGREDIENTS

4 ounces cream cheese with garden vegetables, softened

2 cups water

1 large egg

1 teaspoon grated lemon peel

GOODIES

2 tablespoons olive oil

1/2 cup chopped onion

Lightly seasoned muffins go with everything from salads and pastas to casseroles and egg dishes. So I was delighted when Kraft introduced its Philadelphia Brand Cream Cheese with Garden Vegetables. Almost simultaneously, a number of other manufacturers introduced similar products. You can use any of them in these muffins.

1. Preheat the oven to 400°F.

2. Sift the first six dry ingredients together in a large bowl, then add the remaining dry ingredients and stir to combine.

3. To prepare the goodie mixture, heat the olive oil in a skillet over medium heat. Add the onion, and cook until soft—about 5 minutes. Remove from the heat and let cool to room temperature.

4. Whisk the wet ingredients in a medium bowl or blend in a food processor. Add the goodie mixture and stir to combine.

5. Pour the wet mixture into the dry ingredients. Stir just until mixed. *Do not overstir.*

6. Spoon the batter into a greased or papered muffin tin. Fill each cup nearly to the top.

7. Bake for 15 to 20 minutes.

8. Cool the muffins at least 10 minutes before removing from the tin.

Hushpuppy Muffins

YIELD
12
MUFFINS

Hushpuppies are a regional specialty in the South. These deep-fried balls of cornbread are commonly enjoyed with pork barbecue or seafood. It's not unusual to hear heated arguments over the best way to make them. In addition to the cornmeal, hushpuppies can be made with whole kernel corn, sautéed onions, or both. It's all according to taste. Use your favorite cornmeal—white, yellow, or blue—and enjoy these muffins with a fish dinner or big pot of pinto beans.

DRY INGREDIENTS

1 $\frac{1}{4}$ cups white or yellow cornmeal

$\frac{3}{4}$ cup unbleached white flour

$\frac{1}{2}$ cup whole wheat flour

$\frac{1}{4}$ cup sugar

1 $\frac{1}{2}$ teaspoons baking powder

1 teaspoon baking soda

$\frac{1}{4}$ teaspoon sea salt

WET INGREDIENTS

1 $\frac{1}{4}$ cups milk

1 cup sour cream

1 large egg

GOODIES

1 tablespoon light margarine

$\frac{1}{4}$ cup finely chopped onion

1 cup white or yellow corn kernels

1. Preheat the oven to 400°F.

2. Sift the dry ingredients together in a large bowl.

3. To prepare the goodie mixture, melt the margarine in a small skillet over medium heat. Add the chopped onion and cook until soft—about 5 minutes. Remove from the heat, add the corn, and stir well.

4. Whisk the wet ingredients in a medium bowl or blend in a food processor. Add the goodie mixture and stir to combine.

5. Pour the wet mixture into the dry ingredients. Stir just until mixed. *Do not overstir.*

6. Spoon the batter into a greased or papered muffin tin. Fill each cup nearly to the top.

7. Bake for 15 to 20 minutes.

8. Cool the muffins at least 10 minutes before removing from the tin.

Jewish Rye Muffins

Somewhere in my distant past, I seem to recall seeing ten- to twelve-foot loaves of Jewish rye bread displayed in a bakery window. I remember watching the salespeople slice individual loaves from these "mother loaves," while salivating customers waited for their numbers to be called. The aroma of caraway and rye filled the room, and happy faces warmed the heart. I wanted to warm hearts, too, so I created my Jewish Rye Muffins. Let me know if I have succeeded.

**YIELD
12
MUFFINS**

DRY INGREDIENTS

1 ½ cups rye flour

½ cup whole wheat pastry flour

½ cup whole wheat flour

½ cup unbleached white flour

1 tablespoon baking powder

½ teaspoon baking soda

½ teaspoon sea salt

WET INGREDIENTS

1 ½ cups water

¼ cup canola oil

1 large egg

2 tablespoons honey, warmed

GOODIES

½ cup rye flakes

1 ½ tablespoons caraway seeds

1 cup boiling water

1. Preheat the oven to 400°F.

2. Sift the dry ingredients together in a large bowl.

3. To prepare the goodie mixture, place the rye flakes in a food processor or blender, and grind to a coarse meal. Transfer the rye meal to a medium bowl. Add the caraway seeds, and cover with the boiling water. Set aside and let cool to room temperature.

4. Whisk the wet ingredients together in a small bowl or blend in a food processor. Add the goodie mixture and stir to combine.

5. Pour the wet mixture into the dry ingredients. Stir just until mixed. *Do not overstir.*

6. Spoon the batter into a greased or papered muffin tin. Fill each cup nearly to the top.

7. Bake for 15 to 20 minutes.

8. Cool the muffins at least 10 minutes before removing from the tin.

Mama Mia Muffins

**YIELD
12
MUFFINS**

Garlic has a permanent place in my kitchen. This "Italian caviar" makes everything taste great (except cherry cheesecake and pecan pie). And garlic brings a miraculous healing quality to food. It helps relieve cold and asthma symptoms, aid digestion, soothe poison ivy, and pickle pimples. Basically garlic bread in a muffin, these Mama Mia Muffins go with just about everything. Enjoy them as you would garlic bread. Don't you think "Mama Mia Muffins" has a nice ring to it?

1. Preheat the oven to 400°F.

2. Sift together all the dry ingredients, except the Parmesan cheese, in a large bowl. Then add the cheese and stir to combine.

3. Whisk the wet ingredients in a medium bowl or blend in a food processor. Add the goodies and stir to combine.

4. Pour the wet mixture into the dry ingredients. Stir just until mixed. *Do not overstir.*

5. Spoon the batter into a greased or papered muffin tin. Fill each cup nearly to the top. Top each cup of batter with a pinch of grated Parmesan, taking care to sprinkle it evenly over each cup. Too much topping piled high in the middle will prevent the muffins from rising properly. Sprinkle with paprika.

6. Bake for 15 to 20 minutes.

7. Cool the muffins at least 10 minutes before removing from the tin.

DRY INGREDIENTS

$2\frac{1}{2}$ cups whole wheat pastry flour

$\frac{1}{2}$ cup unbleached white flour

1 tablespoon baking powder

$\frac{1}{4}$ teaspoon sea salt

$\frac{1}{2}$ teaspoon paprika

$\frac{3}{4}$ cup grated Parmesan cheese

WET INGREDIENTS

$1\frac{3}{4}$ cups vegetable broth

$\frac{1}{4}$ cup olive oil

1 large egg

GOODIES

5 cloves garlic, minced

1 tablespoon dried basil

1 teaspoon dried oregano

TOPPING

$\frac{1}{4}$ cup grated Parmesan cheese

Paprika

YIELD
12
MUFFINS

Mexicali Corn Muffins

DRY INGREDIENTS

I cup yellow cornmeal

I cup unbleached
white flour

$1/2$ cup whole wheat flour

I tablespoon baking
powder

$1/4$ teaspoon sea salt

WET INGREDIENTS

$1 1/2$ cups buttermilk

$1/4$ cup olive oil

I large egg

I tablespoon honey

GOODIES

$3/4$ cup grated sharp cheddar
or Monterey jack cheese

$3/4$ cup white or yellow
corn kernels

4-ounce can chopped
jalapeño peppers,
well drained

4-ounce jar chopped
red pimentos,
well drained

Here's a real crowd-pleasing corn muffin—one that is excellent to serve at family get-togethers and potluck meals. It goes well with just about everything—egg dishes, tomato casseroles, Mexican bean dishes, and even Indian curries. To make these muffins even easier to bake, buy the peppers and pimentos already chopped and the cheese grated.

1. Preheat the oven to 400°F.

2. Sift the dry ingredients together in a large bowl.

3. Whisk the wet ingredients in a medium bowl or blend in a food processor. Add the goodies and stir to combine.

4. Pour the wet mixture into the dry ingredients. Stir just until mixed. *Do not overstir.*

5. Spoon the batter into a greased or papered muffin tin. Fill each cup nearly to the top.

6. Bake for 15 to 20 minutes.

7. Cool the muffins at least 10 minutes before removing from the tin.

Nickerpumpel Muffins

YIELD
12
MUFFINS

You may not recognize these. They are Pumpernickel—spelled "crosswise." It's the way I used to say it when I was a kid—nickerpumpel. The darker the molasses and the darker the rye flour you use, the darker your Nickerpumpel Muffins will be. For slightly richer dough, substitute 1 cup buttermilk and $\frac{1}{2}$ cup water for the $1\frac{1}{2}$ cups milk. These muffins are great with a bowl of baked beans, or warm from the oven and drizzled with honey.

1. Preheat the oven to 400°F.

2. Sift together all the dry ingredients, except the caraway seeds, in a large bowl. Then add the caraway seeds and toss.

3. Whisk the wet ingredients together in a medium bowl or blend in a food processor. Be sure the molasses is well blended.

4. Pour the wet ingredients into the dry ingredients. Stir just until mixed. *Do not overstir.*

5. Spoon the batter into a greased or papered muffin tin. Fill each cup nearly to the top.

6. Top each muffin with a sprinkling of cornmeal.

7. Bake for 15 to 20 minutes.

8. Cool the muffins at least 10 minutes before removing from the tin

DRY INGREDIENTS

1 cup whole wheat pastry flour

1 cup dark rye flour

$\frac{1}{2}$ cup buckwheat flour

$\frac{1}{4}$ cup yellow cornmeal

$\frac{1}{4}$ cup soy flour

1 tablespoon baking powder

1 teaspoon baking soda

$\frac{1}{2}$ teaspoon sea salt

1 tablespoon caraway seeds

WET INGREDIENTS

$1\frac{1}{2}$ cups milk

$\frac{1}{4}$ cup canola oil

$\frac{1}{4}$ cup molasses

1 large egg

1 teaspoon grated orange peel

TOPPING

$\frac{1}{8}$ cup yellow cornmeal

YIELD
12
MUFFINS

DRY INGREDIENTS

1 1/2 cup whole wheat pastry flour

1 cup whole wheat flour

1/2 cup unbleached white flour

2 teaspoons baking powder

1/4 teaspoon sea salt

1/2 cup grated Parmesan cheese

WET INGREDIENTS

1 cup vegetable broth

1 cup buttermilk

1/4 cup olive oil

1 large egg

2 teaspoons honey

GOODIES

2 cloves garlic, minced

1/2 cup chopped fresh basil

1/4 cup chopped roasted walnuts

Pesto Muffins

What do you do when you can't decide between pasta with tomato sauce and pasta with pesto sauce? It's a dilemma, isn't it? I realize that sometimes I have to have both. With my Pesto Muffins, I can enjoy pasta with tomato sauce and have my pesto on the side. Try to use fresh basil in these muffins. If you have your own favorite pesto sauce, you can use it (1 cup) in place of the goodies—but if it contains Parmesan cheese, you may want to adjust the cheese amount in the dry ingredients.

1. Preheat the oven to 400°F.

2. Sift together all the dry ingredients, except the Parmesan cheese, in a large bowl. Then add the cheese and stir to combine.

3. Whisk the wet ingredients in a medium bowl or blend in a food processor. Add the goodies and stir to combine.

4. Pour the wet mixture into the dry ingredients. Stir just until mixed. *Do not overstir.*

5. Spoon the batter into a greased or papered muffin tin. Fill each cup nearly to the top.

6. Bake for 15 to 20 minutes.

7. Cool the muffins at least 10 minutes before removing from the tin.

Eat No Muffin Before Its Time

Sascha is always excited to see me. When I drive into the back yard, she races back and forth, back and forth within the walls of the chain link fence that frames her territory—all the while howling and barking and letting the entire neighborhood know that I've returned. If I spend too much time gathering my things before getting out of the car, Sascha goes bananas. She's got so much energy stored up from the few hours I've been away that she can't bear to wait another second before giving me a smooch and letting me stroke her belly. She is impatience on four legs and covered in fur.

When it comes to waiting to enjoy muffins, however, Sascha puts on another face. While I am certain that she has no real understanding of time and calendars and schedules, when I enter the kitchen each Thursday morning, I believe Sascha knows it is baking day and she becomes the mistress of forbearance. Like a centurion patiently guarding his post, she assumes her position in the back foyer at the bottom of the stairs. From this vantage point, she can see my every move and is ready to jump up the instant I reach for her bowl to give her a sample of a freshly baked muffin. Until that time, she waits, waits, waits, all morning long—stirring only to guard me against the letter carrier, sanitation workers, or other threats to my safety.

Given her obvious love of muffins, you would think that when the muffin appears in her bowl, Sascha would wolf it down with a passion. Most of the time she does just that. However I've noticed that if I offer her a bit of muffin before it is fully cooled, she sniffs it, looks at me a bit puzzled, sniffs it again, and walks away. In a few minutes, she returns to check the fare. If by then it has cooled, she devours it in her usual style.

I find this an amazing display of wisdom and self-control. When it comes to eating muffins, Sascha has more sense than I do. It took me several bellyaches from eating muffins that were too hot before I learned the appropriate control. Sascha seemed to know instinctively that muffins just don't settle right unless they are fully cooled first. No matter how wonderful the anticipated pleasure, she waits and waits, and eats no muffin before its time.

Seedy Muffins

YIELD
12
MUFFINS

DRY INGREDIENTS

1 ½ cups whole wheat pastry flour

1 cup unbleached white flour

½ cup rye flour

1 tablespoon soy flour

2 teaspoons baking powder

1 teaspoon baking soda

¼ teaspoon black pepper

WET INGREDIENTS

1 ¾ cups milk

½ cup tahini

¼ cup canola oil

1 large egg

2 tablespoons honey

GOODIES

¼ cup roasted sunflower seeds

2 tablespoons caraway seeds

1 tablespoon hulled sesame seeds

1 tablespoon poppy seeds

1 teaspoon sea salt

2 tablespoons canola oil

4 cloves garlic, minced

There are bagels and there are bagels. A "real" bagel starts with a wholesome dough foundation and ends with a sprinkling of one kind of seed or another. For me, the ultimate bagel is alive and flourishing in a bagel shop that I frequent. It's called an "Everything Bagel" because, like these muffins, it has everything one could possibly want in a "real" bagel—poppy seeds, sesame seeds, and caraway seeds, with a touch of garlic.

1. Preheat the oven to 400°F.

2. Sift the dry ingredients together in a large bowl.

3. To prepare the goodie mixture, grind the sunflower, caraway, sesame, and poppy seeds in a food processor (you can also use a hand-operated mill or a mortar and pestle). Add the remaining goodie ingredients and pulse a few more times. Reserve ¼ cup of this mixture to top the muffins (see Step 5). Add the remaining mixture to the dry ingredients and stir to combine.

4. Whisk the wet ingredients in a medium bowl or blend in a food processor. Pour the wet ingredients into the dry mixture. Stir just until mixed. *Do not overstir.*

5. Spoon the batter into a greased or papered muffin tin. Fill each cup nearly to the top. Top each cup of batter with a large pinch of the reserved goodie mixture, taking care to sprinkle it evenly over each cup. Too much topping piled high in the middle will prevent the muffins from rising properly.

6. Bake for 15 to 20 minutes.

7. Cool the muffins at least 10 minutes before removing from the tin.

Spanakopita Muffins

YIELD
12
MUFFINS

Perhaps more than any other ethnic group, the Greeks enjoy spinach. Spanakopita is a spinach pie of sorts, enhanced with feta cheese and nutmeg. Spinach-stuffed croissants and little spinach pies are takeoffs of this Greek classic. Just thinking about them makes my mouth water. I had to give Spanakopita Muffins a try. And am I glad I did! Make it easy on yourself and buy frozen chopped spinach. Once the spinach is defrosted, drain it well by squeezing out the excess water.

DRY INGREDIENTS

1 ½ cups whole wheat flour

1 cup unbleached white flour

1 tablespoon baking powder

WET INGREDIENTS

1 ½ cups vegetable broth

¼ cup olive oil

1 large egg

GOODIES

1 cup crumbled feta cheese

½ cup cottage cheese

½ cup firmly packed chopped spinach

2 cloves garlic, minced

1 tablespoon honey, warmed

¼ teaspoon ground mace

1. Preheat the oven to 400°F.

2. Sift the dry ingredients together in a large bowl.

3. Whisk the wet ingredients together in a medium bowl or blend in a food processor. Add the goodies and stir by hand (do not use a blender or food processor) to combine.

5. Pour the wet mixture into the dry ingredients. Stir just until mixed. *Do not overstir.*

6. Spoon the batter into a greased or papered muffin tin. Fill each cup nearly to the top.

7. Bake for 15 to 20 minutes.

8. Cool the muffins at least 10 minutes before removing from the tin.

YIELD
14
MUFFINS

DRY INGREDIENTS

1 ½ cups whole wheat flour

1 cup unbleached white flour

1 ½ teaspoons baking powder

1 teaspoons baking powder

¼ teaspoon sea salt

WET INGREDIENTS

1 cup tomato juice

¾ cup milk

¼ cup olive oil

2 teaspoons honey

1 large egg

GOODIES

½ cup sun-dried tomatoes

¾ cup boiling water

4 ounces hot, spicy soysage (1 ¼ cups)

1 tablespoon olive oil

¾ cup grated mozzarella cheese

1 clove minced garlic

1 tablespoon fennel seed

½ teaspoon dried oregano

Soysage Pizza Muffins

Some of my happiest childhood memories include sitting in Grandma's kitchen while she simmered tomato sauce for pasta and pizza. She always included homemade sausage with lots of garlic and fennel. The aroma was outrageous, and the flavor . . . ! Since those days, my diet has changed and I use soysage instead of sausage in my tomato sauce, but I still add plenty of the fennel that was so attractive to me as a child. As it did in Grandma's sauce, fennel makes these Soysage Pizza Muffins one-of-a-kind.

1. To prepare the goodie mixture, first cover the sun-dried tomatoes with boiling water and let soak about 20 minutes. Drain the tomatoes and chop into pea-sized bits. Place in a medium bowl and set aside.

2. Crumble the soysage in a medium skillet over medium heat. Add the olive oil, and sauté until lightly browned. Place the soysage on paper towels to absorb any excess oil, then add to the sun-dried tomatoes along with the remaining goodie ingredients. Stir to combine.

3. Preheat the oven to 400°F

4. Sift the dry ingredients together in a large bowl.

5. Whisk the wet ingredients in a medium bowl or blend in a food processor. Add to the goodie mixture and stir to combine.

6. Pour the wet mixture into the dry ingredients. Stir just until mixed. *Do not overstir.*

7. Spoon the batter into a greased or papered muffin tin. Fill each cup nearly to the top. Top each cup of batter with a scant tablespoon of mozzarella, taking care to sprinkle it evenly over each cup. Too much topping piled high in the middle will prevent the muffins from rising properly.

8. Bake for 15 to 20 minutes.

9. Cool the muffins at least 10 minutes before removing from the tin.

TOPPING
3/4 cup grated mozzarella cheese

YIELD
12
MUFFINS

DRY INGREDIENTS

2 cups whole wheat pastry flour

$^1/_2$ cup brown rice flour

I tablespoon baking powder

WET INGREDIENTS

$^3/_4$ cup buttermilk

$^3/_4$ cup vegetable broth

$^1/_8$ cup canola oil

I tablespoon toasted sesame oil

I tablespoon rice syrup, warmed

I tablespoon soy sauce

I large egg

GOODIES

15 water chestnuts, chopped

15 dried apricots, chopped

6 tablespoons chopped celery

2 tablespoons chopped scallion (about 2)

I tablespoon finely chopped fresh ginger root, or I $^1/_2$ teaspoons ground

I clove garlic, minced

Spring Roll Muffins

What we call an "egg roll" is called a "spring roll" in China because it is served during the spring festivals. I like mine crispy (but not greasy) and smothered in apricot duck sauce. But what I really like is the combination of flavors in each bite. "Why not bring this same combination to a muffin?" I thought. That way, I won't have to go to Chinese restaurants to enjoy these flavors. Sound crazy? Confucius says, "Try these before you turn up your nose." Mmm. Mmm!

1. Preheat the oven to 400°F.

2. Sift the dry ingredients together in a large bowl.

3. Whisk the wet ingredients in a medium bowl or blend in a food processor. Add the goodies and stir to combine.

4. Pour the wet mixture into the dry ingredients. Stir just until mixed. *Do not overstir.*

5. Spoon the batter into a greased or papered muffin tin. Fill each cup nearly to the top.

6. Bake for 15 to 20 minutes.

7. Cool the muffins at least 10 minutes before removing from the tin.

Steven's Sun-Dried Tomato Muffins

**YIELD
14
MUFFINS**

My friend Steven—the inspiration for this recipe—has a knack for making even the simplest dishes look and taste elegant. Years ago, he served a pizza that had a deep, deep tomato flavor, which I suspected came from the red mushy chunks that looked like pimentos. I learned they were sun-dried tomatoes. I also discovered that it takes as many as eighteen pounds of fresh tomatoes to make one pound of sun-dried. No wonder they're so rich!

1. To prepare the goodie mixture, first cover the sun-dried tomatoes with boiling water and let soak about 20 minutes. Drain the tomatoes and chop into pea-sized bits. Place in a medium bowl along with the remaining goodie ingredients. Stir to combine.

2. Preheat the oven to 400°F.

3. Sift the dry ingredients together in a large bowl.

4. Whisk the wet ingredients in a medium bowl or blend in a food processor. Add to the goodie mixture and stir to combine.

5. Pour the wet mixture into the dry ingredients. Stir just until mixed. *Do not overstir.*

6. Spoon the batter into a greased or papered muffin tin. Fill each cup nearly to the top.

7. Bake for 15 to 20 minutes.

8. Cool the muffins at least 10 minutes before removing from the tin.

DRY INGREDIENTS

1 1/2 cups whole wheat flour

1 cup unbleached white flour

2 teaspoons baking powder

1 teaspoon baking soda

1/4 teaspoon black pepper

WET INGREDIENTS

1 3/4 cups tomato juice

1/4 cup olive oil

1 large egg

1 tablespoon honey

GOODIES

1/2 cup sun-dried tomatoes

3/4 cup hot water

3/4 cup pine nuts or chopped walnuts

2 cloves garlic, minced

1/2 cup grated Parmesan cheese

1/2 cup firmly packed chopped spinach

1 tablespoon dried oregano

1 tablespoon dried basil

Stuffin' Muffins

YIELD
12–14
MUFFINS

DRY INGREDIENTS

1 cup unbleached white flour

$^3/_4$ cup whole wheat flour

2 teaspoons baking powder

1 teaspoon baking soda

$^1/_4$ teaspoon sea salt

1 cup coarse bread crumbs

WET INGREDIENTS

1 cup vegetable broth

$^3/_4$ cup milk

$^1/_4$ cup olive oil

1 large egg

1 tablespoon honey

GOODIES

$^1/_4$ cup grated sharp cheddar cheese

$^1/_4$ cup chopped celery

$^1/_4$ cup chopped onion

$^1/_4$ cup coarsely chopped walnuts

$^1/_4$ cup roasted sunflower seeds

$^1/_4$ cup raisins

2 teaspoons chopped fresh parsley, or 1 teaspoon dried

2 cloves garlic, minced

$^1/_2$ teaspoon rubbed sage

$^1/_2$ teaspoon ground thyme

In an episode of Dennis the Menace, *Dennis said, "No more turkey, please, but I'd like some more of the bread it ate." I can relate! I'm a bread-stuffing lover from way back. Bread stuffing in a muffin? Who could ask for more? Be sure to use only coarse bread crumbs prepared from leftover bread. If you don't have any, substitute $^3/_4$ cup additional flour for the bread crumbs. And don't use heavy store-bought bread crumbs, as they'll make the muffins too heavy. Serve these Stuffin' Muffins as you would stuffin' stuffin.'*

1. Preheat the oven to 400°F.

2. Sift together all the dry ingredients, except the bread crumbs, in a large bowl. Then add the bread crumbs and toss.

3. Whisk the wet ingredients in a medium bowl or blend in a food processor. Add the goodies and stir to combine.

4. Pour the wet mixture into the dry ingredients. Stir just until mixed. *Do not overstir.*

5. Spoon the batter into a greased or papered muffin tin. Fill each cup nearly to the top.

6. Bake for 15 to 20 minutes.

7. Cool the muffins at least 10 minutes before removing from the tin.

Sun-Dried Tomato Corn Muffins with Cumin

YIELD
11–12
MUFFINS

One evening, my friends Randy and Steven served sun-dried tomato bread with one of their fabulous dinners. It was reddish in color and contained an occasional cumin seed to set things off. We sat there, savoring the flavors, commenting on what we liked, and determining what we might do differently if we baked the bread. "Corn," I said. "It wants corn." Thus was born my Sun-Dried Tomato Corn Muffins with Cumin.

DRY INGREDIENTS

1 $\frac{1}{2}$ cup unbleached white flour

1 cup yellow or white cornmeal

$\frac{1}{2}$ cup whole wheat flour

2 teaspoons baking soda

$\frac{1}{2}$ teaspoon baking powder

$\frac{1}{4}$ teaspoon sea salt

$\frac{1}{4}$ teaspoon ground black pepper

WET INGREDIENTS

1 cup tomato juice

1 cup buttermilk

1 tablespoon olive oil

1 tablespoon honey

1 large egg

GOODIES

$\frac{1}{2}$ cup sun-dried tomatoes

$\frac{1}{2}$ cup boiling water

1 teaspoon whole cumin seeds

1. To prepare the goodie mixture, first cover the sun-dried tomatoes with boiling water and let soak about 20 minutes. Drain the tomatoes and chop into pea-sized bits. Place in a medium bowl along with the remaining goodie ingredients. Stir to combine.

2. Preheat the oven to 400°F.

3. Sift the dry ingredients together in a large bowl.

4. Whisk the wet ingredients in a medium bowl or blend in a food processor. Add the goodie mixture and stir to combine.

5. Pour the wet mixture into the dry ingredients. Stir just until mixed. *Do not overstir.*

6. Spoon the batter into a greased or papered muffin tin. Fill each cup nearly to the top.

7. Bake for 15 to 20 minutes.

8. Cool the muffins at least 10 minutes before removing from the tin.

YIELD 10–12 MUFFINS

DRY INGREDIENTS

1 1/2 cups whole wheat flour

1/2 cup whole wheat pastry flour

1/2 cup unbleached white flour

1 1/2 teaspoons baking soda

1/2 teaspoon baking powder

1/4 teaspoon sea salt

1/4 teaspoon ground black pepper

WET INGREDIENTS

1 cup tomato juice

3/4 cup water

1 large egg

1 tablespoon olive oil

1 tablespoon honey

GOODIES

1/2 cup sun-dried tomatoes

3/4 cup boiling water

1/2 cup chopped fresh basil

1 clove garlic, minced

Tomato Basil Muffins

There's nothing like the taste of fresh basil. Lucky for me, my friends Diana and Nancy have a backyard that overflows with basil plants, and they let me help myself whenever I want. I saturate these muffins with basil, and encourage you to also. Pack as may leaves as you can fit into a half cup, then either chop them by hand or let your food processor do the work. Between the basil and the sun-dried tomatoes, these muffins are bursting with flavor—a great compliment to any pasta dish or salad.

1. To prepare the goodie mixture, first cover the sun-dried tomatoes with boiling water and let soak about 20 minutes. Drain the tomatoes and chop into pea-sized bits. Place in a medium bowl along with the remaining goodie ingredients. Stir to combine.

2. Preheat the oven to 400°F.

3. Sift the dry ingredients together in a large bowl.

4. Whisk the wet ingredients in a medium bowl or blend in a food processor. Add the goodie mixture and stir to combine.

5. Pour the wet mixture into the dry ingredients. Stir just until mixed. *Do not overstir.*

6. Spoon the batter into a greased or papered muffin tin. Fill each cup nearly to the top.

7. Bake for 15 to 20 minutes.

8. Cool the muffins at least 10 minutes before removing from the tin.

Waldorf Muffins

Waldorf salad is one of my favorite fruity accompaniments for holiday meals. The combination of apples, raisins, celery, and nuts captures everything that comes to mind when I think of fall holiday menus. I use dried and fresh apples as well as apple juice concentrate to give depth to the apple-ness of these Waldorf Muffins, which are great throughout the year. Bring them on summer picnics, or to the beach or pool. They are also great at Fourth of July backyard picnics.

1. Preheat the oven to 400°F.

2. Sift the dry ingredients together in a large bowl.

3. Whisk the wet ingredients in a medium bowl or blend in a food processor. Add the goodies and stir to combine.

4. Pour the wet mixture into the dry ingredients. Stir just until mixed. *Do not overstir.*

5. Spoon the batter into a greased or papered muffin tin. Fill each cup nearly to the top.

6. Bake for 15 to 20 minutes.

7. Cool the muffins at least 10 minutes before removing from the tin.

YIELD
12
MUFFINS

DRY INGREDIENTS
1 1/2 cups whole wheat flour

1 cup unbleached white flour

2 teaspoons baking powder

1 teaspoon baking soda

1/4 teaspoon sea salt

WET INGREDIENTS
1 1/2 cups milk

1/2 cup apple juice concentrate

1/4 cup canola oil

1 large egg

1 teaspoon grated lemon peel

GOODIES
3/4 cup finely chopped celery

1/2 cup raisins

1/2 cup coarsely chopped roasted walnuts

1/2 cup chopped fresh apples

1/4 cup chopped dried apples

5. **Holiday,**Special **Occasion,**and **Good**Time**Muffins**

For now I am in a holiday humour.

—WILLIAM SHAKESPEARE, *AS YOU LIKE IT*

I am rarely without an excuse to bake muffins; breathing is excuse enough. But, as you can imagine, if I bake muffins every time I take a breath, I will feel a tad obsessed before long. That's why I love the holidays and special occasions—times that are filled with parties, family gatherings, friendly visits, and presents! These times give me zillions of excuses to bake. Consider the following:

• The holiday season means parties, lots of parties—office parties, club parties, school parties. Whatever the event, whether a pot-luck dinner, an elegant buffet, or a sit-down meal, you can make delicious holiday muffins to suit the occasion. My friend Susan loves to bring muffins to parties. She says they are always the most popular offering, and people remember who brought them! (P.S. You don't have to limit yourself to the muffin recipes in this chapter. All of my muffins are great for parties.)

- Holidays are a time for "drop-in" visits. Bake muffins to have "a little something" to serve unexpected guests. Start baking at Halloween and go right on through the New Year. I bet you will use every muffin you bake.

- Muffins make wonderful presents—for teachers, family, friends, and holiday hosts. Fill a nicely decorated basket with a dozen muffins. Add a tub of muffin butter or spread from Chapter 8, and you've got an unforgettable gift. Who doesn't like baked goods—especially during the holidays?

- Muffins let you "prepare" for unexpected gifts. Keep several dozen (individually wrapped and labeled) in the freezer just in case someone arrives with an unexpected gift for *you*!

Throughout the year, I search for interesting baskets at wicker warehouses, import shops, and thrift stores. I keep an assortment on hand, and whenever I need a gift, I fill one with muffins. I also usually include a card with instructions for freezing and reheating (see page 28).

Whether you make them to stuff stockings or to stuff faces, muffins are a most welcome holiday treat. But what about the rest of the year? What about the birthdays, un-birthdays, and other holidays? Although I created my "Holiday, Special Occasion, and Good Time Muffins" with the fall and winter holidays in mind, you can bake them for any occasion, no matter what time of the year.

Cranberry-Orange Muffins

YIELD
12
MUFFINS

DRY INGREDIENTS

2 cups whole wheat pastry flour

$1/2$ cup unbleached white flour

2 teaspoons baking powder

I teaspoon baking soda

$1/4$ teaspoon sea salt

WET INGREDIENTS

I cup milk

$1/2$ cup apple juice concentrate

$1/4$ cup canola oil

I cup all-fruit orange marmalade

I large egg

2 tablespoons grated orange peel

I teaspoon vanilla extract

GOODIES

I cup chopped cranberries

I cup coarsely chopped roasted walnuts

When I was very young, my oldest sister, Betty, introduced our family to cranberry nut loaf. My other sisters and I were dazzled to see cranberries in bread (we thought they came only in cranberry sauce). We loved the bread and quickly made it a holiday tradition. More recently, I created a cranberry-orange-walnut relish that is fast becoming another tradition. These muffins are a spin-off of Betty's bread and my relish. Try them with Lemony Lemon Spread (page 190).

1. Preheat the oven to 400°F.

2. Sift the dry ingredients together in a large bowl. Add the goodies and toss to coat

3. Whisk the wet ingredients in a medium bowl or blend in a food processor. Pour the wet ingredients into the dry mixture. Stir just until mixed. *Do not overstir.*

4. Spoon the batter into a greased or papered muffin tin. Fill each cup nearly to the top.

5. Bake for 15 to 20 minutes.

6. Cool the muffins at least 10 minutes before removing from the tin.

Amaretto Muffins

**YIELD
12
MUFFINS**

DRY INGREDIENTS

1 cup whole wheat flour

$3/4$ cup unbleached white flour

$3/4$ cup barley flour

$1/2$ cup sugar

$1 1/2$ teaspoons baking powder

1 teaspoon baking soda

$1/4$ teaspoon sea salt

WET INGREDIENTS

1 cup buttermilk

$1/2$ cup water

1 large egg

$1/4$ cup honey

$1 1/2$ teaspoons amaretto flavoring

GOODIES

$3/4$ cup dark sweet cherries, pitted and chopped

TOPPING

$1/2$ cup sliced almonds

1 tablespoon pearl sugar

3 dark sweet cherries, cut in quarters

I had wanted to make an amaretto-flavored muffin for some time, but I was never able to get the flavoring quite right. That is, not until flavored coffees became popular. That's when little bottles of interesting flavors— amaretto, Irish cream, cappuccino, toasted pecan—began appearing on grocery store shelves. Just a drop or two turns ordinary coffee into a coffee-bar masterpiece. I used this type of flavoring in these muffins.

1. Preheat the oven to 400°F.

2. Sift the dry ingredients together in a large bowl. Add the goodies and toss to coat.

3. Whisk the wet ingredients in a medium bowl or blend in a food processor. Pour the wet ingredients into the dry mixture. Stir just until mixed. *Do not overstir.*

4. Spoon the batter into a greased or papered muffin tin. Fill each cup nearly to the top. Top each cup of batter with a large pinch of sliced almonds and a sprinkling of pearl sugar. Crown with a cherry quarter.

5. Bake for 15 to 20 minutes.

6. Cool the muffins at least 10 minutes before removing from the tin.

Anise Orange Muffins

Licorice-flavored anise has always been part of my diet. When I was a baby, my mom gave me anise-flavored zwieback cookies to sooth my gums as I teethed. (She also rubbed cognac on them—but that's another story!) As I grew older, my love of anise resulted in a devotion to Good 'n Plenty candy, anisette biscotti, and, of course, my Anise Orange Muffins. Why did I include the orange in this recipe? That's easy—the two flavors taste great together.

YIELD
12
MUFFINS

DRY INGREDIENTS

1 1/2 cups whole wheat flour

1 1/2 cups unbleached white flour

2 teaspoons baking powder

1 teaspoon baking soda

1/4 teaspoon sea salt

1/2 teaspoon ground cardamom

WET INGREDIENTS

1 cup cottage cheese

3/4 cup milk

1/2 cup honey

1/4 cup canola oil

1 large egg

3 tablespoon grated orange peel

GOODIES

2 1/2 tablespoons anise seeds

1. Preheat the oven to 400°F.

2. Sift the dry ingredients together in a large bowl.

3. Grind the anise seeds in a food processor (you can also use a hand-operated mill or a mortar and pestle). Add the seeds to the dry ingredients and stir to combine.

4. Whisk the wet ingredients in a medium bowl. Do not use a blender or food processor. Pour the wet ingredients into the dry mixture. Stir just until mixed. *Do not overstir.*

5. Spoon the batter into a greased or papered muffin tin. Fill each cup nearly to the top.

6. Bake for 15 to 20 minutes.

7. Cool the muffins at least 10 minutes before removing from the tin.

YIELD
12
MUFFINS

DRY INGREDIENTS

1 cup whole wheat flour

$3/4$ cup unbleached white flour

$3/4$ cup barley flour

$3/4$ cup light brown sugar

1 $1/2$ teaspoons baking powder

1 teaspoon baking soda

$1/4$ teaspoon sea salt

WET INGREDIENTS

3 ripe bananas, mashed (1 $1/2$ cups)

$3/4$ cup milk

$1/2$ cup coffee, cooled

1 large egg

2 teaspoons vanilla extract

GOODIES

$1/2$ cup mini semi-sweet chocolate chips

TOPPING

1 large egg white

$1/2$ cup coarsely chopped roasted walnuts

Banana Nut Fudge Muffins

Whenever I try to enjoy a hot fudge banana split, self-denigrating thoughts like "Why don't you just smear it on your thighs?" get in the way. Then I have to say, "Quiet. I'm trying to focus on the taste buds dancing in my mouth." To mirror the flavors of this luscious dessert, I created these muffins. When I bite into them, I don't hear the critical voices. Perhaps it's because they are so low in fat. Do you think the chatterbox inside our heads may be controlled by a fat meter?

1. Preheat the oven to 400°F.

2. Sift the dry ingredients together in a large bowl. Add the goodies and toss to coat.

3. Whisk the wet ingredients in a medium bowl or blend in a food processor. Pour the wet ingredients into the dry mixture. Stir just until mixed. *Do not overstir.*

4. Spoon the batter into a greased or papered muffin tin. Fill each cup nearly to the top.

5. To prepare the topping, whip the egg white until it forms soft peaks. Add the walnuts and stir to coat completely. Top each cup of batter with topping, taking care to spread it evenly over each cup. Too much topping piled high in the middle will prevent the muffins from rising properly.

6. Bake for 15 to 20 minutes.

7. Cool the muffins at least 10 minutes before removing from the tin.

Bananas Foster Muffins

YIELD
12
MUFFINS

Years ago, my boyfriend and I enjoyed a candlelit dinner in Asheville, North Carolina. With the Blue Ridge Mountains spread majestically across our field of vision, the music of love songs filled the air. Tableside, our waiter set brandy-soaked bananas aflame with a flamboyant gesture. My boyfriend, the Blue Ridge Mountains, love songs, and Bananas Foster. Ah, life is good. Now, with my Bananas Foster Muffins, I can relive that wonderful evening again and again. Ah, life is double good!

1. Preheat the oven to 375°F.

2. Sift the dry ingredients together in a large bowl.

3. Whisk the wet ingredients in a medium bowl or blend in a food processor. Pour the wet ingredients into the dry ingredients. Stir just until mixed. *Do not overstir.*

4. Spoon the batter into a greased or papered muffin tin. Fill each cup nearly to the top. Top each cup of batter with about 1 teaspoon wheat germ, taking care to sprinkle it evenly over each cup. Too much topping piled high in the middle will prevent the muffins from rising properly.

5. Bake for 15 to 20 minutes.

6. Cool the muffins at least 10 minutes before removing from the tin.

DRY INGREDIENTS

1 1/2 cup unbleached white flour

3/4 cup whole wheat pastry flour

1/2 cup whole wheat flour

3/4 cup light brown sugar

1 1/4 teaspoons baking soda

1 teaspoon baking powder

1/4 teaspoon sea salt

WET INGREDIENTS

3 ripe bananas, mashed (1 1/2 cups)

1/2 cup sour cream

1/2 cup milk

1/4 cup canola oil

1 large egg

3 1/2 teaspoons brandy flavoring

1 teaspoon vanilla extract

1 teaspoon grated lemon peel

CRUNCHY TOPPING

3 tablespoons honey crunch wheat germ

Blackberry Cheesecake Muffins

YIELD
12–14
MUFFINS

DRY INGREDIENTS

2 cups whole wheat pastry flour

1/2 cup unbleached white flour

1/2 cup sugar

2 teaspoons baking powder

1 teaspoon baking soda

1/4 teaspoon sea salt

1/4 teaspoon ground nutmeg

WET INGREDIENTS

8 ounces cream cheese, softened

1 1/4 cup milk

1/2 cup sour cream

1 large egg

1 teaspoon vanilla extract

1 teaspoon rum extract

1 teaspoon grated lemon peel

GOODIES

3/4 cup firm fresh blackberries, washed, patted dry, and halved (or 12-ounce frozen package, thawed)

Once upon a time, cheesecake was a simple dessert made from soft cheeses and served plain. Remember that? Before long, we daubed it with blueberries, cherries, and pineapple. We laced it with brandy, layered it with raspberry conserve, and topped it with kiwi and star fruit. It was only a matter of time before someone put blackberries and cheesecake together—pure inspiration for this special occasion muffin.

1. Preheat the oven to 400°F.

2. Sift the dry ingredients together in a large bowl. Add the goodies and toss to coat.

3. Using the purée blade of a food processor, cream the cream cheese and sour cream. Add the remaining wet ingredients and blend. (If you do not have a food processor, use a hand-held mixer at medium speed.)

4. Pour the wet ingredients into the dry mixture. Taking care not to break the blackberries, stir gently just until mixed. *Do not overstir.*

5. Spoon the batter into a greased or papered muffin tin. Fill each cup nearly to the top.

6. Bake for 15 to 20 minutes.

7. Cool the muffins at least 10 minutes before removing from the tin.

Butterscotch Pecan Muffins

YIELD
12–13
MUFFINS

I wanted to create a muffin with the nutty, burnt-sugar flavor of pecan pralines. At first, I made the pralines from scratch, but it was much too labor intensive. Soon thereafter, I discovered butterscotch chips. "Hmm," I thought. "Butterscotch candies are very similar to pralines. Using the chips and the butterscotch syrup would certainly give my muffins that great praline taste without all the fuss." It worked!

1. Preheat the oven to 400°F.

2. Sift the dry ingredients together in a large bowl. Add the goodies and stir to combine.

3. Whisk the wet ingredients in a medium bowl or blend in a food processor. Pour the wet ingredients into the dry mixture. Stir just until mixed. *Do not overstir.*

4. Spoon the batter into a greased or papered muffin tin. Fill each cup nearly to the top. Top each cup of batter with a large pinch of roasted pecans, taking care to sprinkle them evenly over each cup. Too much topping piled high in the middle will prevent the muffins from rising properly.

5. Bake for 15 to 20 minutes.

6. Cool the muffins at least 10 minutes before removing from the tin.

DRY INGREDIENTS

1 $\frac{1}{4}$ cups whole wheat flour

1 $\frac{1}{4}$ cups unbleached white flour

$\frac{1}{2}$ cup dark brown sugar

1 $\frac{1}{2}$ teaspoons baking soda

1 teaspoon baking powder

$\frac{1}{4}$ teaspoon sea salt

WET INGREDIENTS

1 $\frac{1}{4}$ cups milk

$\frac{1}{2}$ cup butterscotch syrup

$\frac{1}{2}$ cup sour cream

1 large egg

1 $\frac{1}{2}$ teaspoons vanilla extract

GOODIES

$\frac{1}{2}$ cup chopped roasted pecans

$\frac{1}{2}$ cup butterscotch chips

TOPPING

$\frac{1}{2}$ cup chopped roasted pecans

YIELD 12 MUFFINS

Caribbean Sweet Potato Gingerbread Muffins

DRY INGREDIENTS

1 ½ cups whole wheat pastry flour

½ cup whole wheat flour

½ cup unbleached white flour

½ cup dark brown sugar

1 ½ teaspoons baking soda

1 teaspoon baking powder

1 teaspoon ground cinnamon

½ teaspoon ground cloves

¼ teaspoon ground nutmeg

¼ teaspoon sea salt

WET INGREDIENTS

1 cup sweet potato purée

1 cup milk

¼ cup molasses

1 large egg

2 teaspoons grated orange peel

1 tablespoon grated fresh ginger root, or 1 ½ teaspoons ground

To make the purée called for in this recipe, first, drain a 16-ounce can of sweet potatoes, reserving the liquid. Then purée the potatoes in a blender or food processor with 1 cup of the reserved liquid—if necessary, add more water to measure this amount. You can also use a fork or potato ricer to mash the potatoes by hand. Use what you need for the recipe and freeze the remaining purée for your next batch. Or make a double batch of muffins now!

1. Preheat the oven to 400°F.

2. Sift the dry ingredients together in a large bowl.

3. Whisk the wet ingredients in a medium bowl or blend in a food processor. Pour the wet ingredients into the dry ingredients. Stir just until mixed. *Do not overstir.*

4. Spoon the batter into a greased or papered muffin tin. Fill each cup nearly to the top.

5. Bake for 15 to 20 minutes.

6. Cool the muffins at least 10 minutes before removing from the tin.

Chocolate-Almond Muffins

One of the things I miss about living in the Northeast is the abundance of fantastic Italian grocery stores and restaurants. I miss the lasagna, the calzones, the cannoli, and the biscotti. I really miss the freshly made biscotti. Imagine my delight when I discovered that my favorite coffee shop began to make them. I immediately sat down to enjoy a chocolate-almond biscotti dunked in a fresh cup of cappuccino. It was this wonderful cookie that inspired my Chocolate-Almond Muffins.

1. Preheat the oven to 400°F.

2. Sift the dry ingredients together in a large bowl. Add the goodies and stir to combine.

3. Whisk the wet ingredients in a medium bowl or blend in a food processor. Pour the wet ingredients into the dry mixture. Stir just until mixed. *Do not overstir.*

4. Spoon the batter into a greased or papered muffin tin. Fill each cup nearly to the top. Top each cup of batter with a large pinch of sliced almonds, taking care to sprinkle them evenly over each cup.

5. Bake for 15 to 20 minutes.

6. Cool the muffins at least 10 minutes before removing from the tin.

YIELD
12
MUFFINS

DRY INGREDIENTS

1 1/2 cups whole wheat flour

1 1/4 cups unbleached white flour

1/4 cup light brown sugar

6 tablespoons cocoa powder

1 1/2 teaspoons baking soda

1 teaspoon baking powder

1/4 teaspoon sea salt

WET INGREDIENTS

1 1/2 cups milk

1/2 cup sour cream

1/4 cup canola oil

1 large egg

2 teaspoons almond extract

1 teaspoon vanilla extract

GOODIES

3/4 cup mini semi-sweet chocolate chips

TOPPING

1/2 cup sliced almonds

Chocolate-Ginger Muffins

YIELD
11–12
MUFFINS

DRY INGREDIENTS

1 1/4 cups unbleached white flour

1/2 cup whole wheat flour

1/2 cup whole wheat pastry flour

1/2 cup brown rice flour

1/2 cup light brown sugar

6 tablespoons cocoa powder

1 teaspoon baking powder

1 teaspoon baking soda

1/4 teaspoon sea salt

WET INGREDIENTS

1 cup buttermilk

3/4 cup water

1/4 cup honey

1/4 cup canola oil

1 large egg

1 1/2 teaspoons vanilla extract

GOODIES

1/4 cup coarsely chopped crystallized ginger

One year, while I was visiting an English monastery, a friend introduced me to chocolate-covered ginger. I loved it! The dark chocolate warmed my palate, while the sting of ginger really got my attention. When I returned home, I introduced it to my family and friends. Despite the fact that no one seemed particularly excited about it (I guess it's an acquired taste), I created Chocolate-Ginger Muffins. You tell me. Is this a fabulous combination, or what?

1. Preheat the oven to 400°F.

2. Sift the dry ingredients together in a large bowl. Add the goodies and toss to coat

3. Whisk the wet ingredients in a medium bowl or blend in a food processor. Pour the wet ingredients into the dry mixture. Stir just until mixed. *Do not overstir.*

4. Spoon the batter into a greased or papered muffin tin. Fill each cup nearly to the top.

5. Bake for 15 to 20 minutes.

6. Cool the muffins at least 10 minutes before removing from the tin.

Chocolate Raspberry Chambord Muffins

YIELD
12
MUFFINS

A few years back, my roommate received a chocolate bourbon cake. Soaked in bourbon, the cake was so rich, we could eat only a thin slice at a time, and it was so moist that it resembled plum pudding. It occurred to me that I could also soak muffins with liquor or liqueur. They would grace any holiday table or serve as the perfect ending to an elegant dinner. Enjoy these chocolate-raspberry flavored gems with a dollop of whipped cream.

1. Preheat the oven to 400°F.

2. Sift the dry ingredients together in a large bowl. Add the goodies and toss to coat.

3. Whisk the wet ingredients in a medium bowl or blend in a food processor. Pour the wet ingredients into the dry mixture. Stir just until mixed, taking care not to break the raspberries. *Do not overstir.*

4. Spoon the batter into a greased or papered muffin tin. Fill each cup nearly to the top.

5. Bake for 15 to 20 minutes.

6. Remove the muffins from the oven and immediately pierce the top of each six or seven times with a skewer or toothpick. Drizzle the liqueur evenly over each muffin.

7. Cool the muffins at least 15 to 20 minutes before removing from the tin.

DRY INGREDIENTS

1 1/4 cups whole wheat flour

1 1/4 cups unbleached white flour

1/2 cup light brown sugar

6 tablespoons cocoa powder

1 1/2 teaspoons baking soda

1 teaspoon baking powder

1/4 teaspoon sea salt

WET INGREDIENTS

1 1/2 cups buttermilk

1/4 cup honey

1/4 cup canola oil

1 large egg

2 teaspoon raspberry flavoring

1 teaspoon vanilla extract

GOODIES

3/4 cup firm fresh raspberries, washed, patted dry, and halved

1/2 cup mini semi-sweet chocolate chips

GLAZE

1/4 cup Chambord, or other raspberry liqueur

YIELD
12
MUFFINS

DRY INGREDIENTS

1 cup whole wheat
pastry flour

1 cup whole wheat flour

$1/2$ cup unbleached
white flour

2 teaspoons baking
powder

1 teaspoon baking
soda

$1/4$ teaspoon sea salt

WET INGREDIENTS

$1 1/2$ cups milk

$1/4$ cup apple juice
concentrate

$1/4$ cup canola oil

1 large egg

2 teaspoons rum
extract

GOODIES

$1/2$ cup flaked coconut

$3/4$ cup crushed pineapple,
well drained

TOPPING

$1/4$ cup flaked coconut

Classic Colada Muffins

These muffins capture that wonderful piña colada blend of tropical flavors right down to the rum. This recipe works best with canned crushed pineapple—fresh is too acidic for baking. Choose pineapple that is packed in its own juice, and be sure to drain it well. For added pineapple flavor, replace the apple juice concentrate with the drained pineapple juice.

1. Preheat the oven to 400°F.

2. Sift the dry ingredients together in a large bowl. Add the goodies and toss to coat

3. Whisk the wet ingredients in a medium bowl or blend in a food processor. Pour the wet ingredients into the dry mixture. Stir just until mixed. *Do not overstir.*

4. Spoon the batter into a greased or papered muffin tin. Fill each cup nearly to the top. Top each cup of batter with a large sprinkling of coconut, taking care to sprinkle it evenly over each cup. Too much topping piled high in the middle will prevent the muffins from rising properly.

5. Bake for 15 to 20 minutes.

6. Cool the muffins at least 10 minutes before removing from the tin.

When All Else Fails,
Follow the Directions

My sister Diane telephoned one day to tell me that her favorite muffins are the Eat-Your-Oatmeal Muffins (page 44). She said she was making a batch just about every other week and loved them. "However," she said, "the kids thought the last batch I made was a little heavy." She wondered why.

"Well," I said, "describe how you made them." I could hear her turning the pages of my book to find the recipe.

"Well, first of all, I guess I better tell you that I didn't have any whole wheat pastry flour, so I used a mixture of whole wheat and white."

"That's fine," I said. "Did you find that you needed to adjust the liquid?"

"Well, yeah—especially to absorb the cereal."

"What cereal?" I asked.

"Oh, I forgot to tell you about that. I ran out of rolled oats, so I pulverized some stale Wheaties."

"I see."

"And then there was the thing with the apples."

"What about the apples?"

"I didn't have any, so I used some canned fruit cocktail instead."

"Diane! Is there anything else you want to tell me?"

"Just the applesauce."

"Huh?"

"You see, I didn't have any apple juice concentrate, so I watered down some applesauce instead."

"Gee, Diane, I wonder why the muffins didn't come out right . . ."

YIELD
12
MUFFINS

DRY INGREDIENTS

1 ½ cups whole wheat flour

1 cup unbleached
white flour

½ cup light brown sugar

6 tablespoons cocoa
powder

1 ¼ teaspoons baking
soda

1 teaspoon baking
powder

¼ teaspoon sea salt

WET INGREDIENTS

1 ¾ cups buttermilk

½ cup honey

¼ cup canola oil

1 large egg

1 ½ teaspoons vanilla
extract

GOODIES

¾ cup mini semi-sweet
chocolate chips

½ cup coarsely chopped
milk chocolate

Double Chocolate
Chocolate Muffins

*According to Debra Waterhouse in her book **Why Women Need Chocolate**, half of all women say they'd choose chocolate over sex any day. She explains that chocolate is about half sugar, which raises serotonin levels and produces a temporary "high." It also contains fat, which boosts those feel-good endorphins. The moral of the story? If you're a woman, skip the sex and try my Double Chocolate Chocolate Muffins. If you're a man who loves a woman, don't bake her my Double Chocolate Chocolate Muffins.*

1. Preheat the oven to 400°F.

2. Sift the dry ingredients together in a large bowl. Add the goodies and stir to combine.

3. Whisk the wet ingredients in a medium bowl or blend in a food processor. Pour the wet ingredients into the dry mixture. Stir just until mixed. *Do not overstir.*

4. Spoon the batter into a greased or papered muffin tin. Fill each cup nearly to the top.

5. Bake for 15 to 20 minutes.

6. Cool the muffins at least 10 minutes before removing from the tin.

Down-to-Earth Date-and-Nut Muffins

YIELD
12
MUFFINS

When I was a Brownie, during a meeting right before Christmas, my troop leaders arrived with baskets of whole dates, bowls of blanched almonds, and bags of finely grated coconut. We were going to make stuffed dates as Christmas presents for our parents. We removed the pit from each date, replaced it with an almond, and then rolled it in coconut. Ugh, I couldn't imagine that anyone was actually going to eat those things. Now, I love them, and created this muffin as a result.

DRY INGREDIENTS

1 1/4 cups whole wheat flour

3/4 cup unbleached white flour

1 teaspoon baking powder

1 teaspoon baking soda

1 1/2 teaspoons ground cinnamon

1/4 teaspoon sea salt

2 tablespoons oat or wheat bran

WET INGREDIENTS

1 1/2 cups buttermilk

1/4 cup honey

1/4 cup molasses

1 large egg

2 teaspoons grated orange peel

1 teaspoon vanilla extract

GOODIES

3/4 cup chopped pitted dates

3/4 cup chopped roasted almonds

3/4 cup flaked coconut

1. Preheat the oven to 400°F.

2. Sift together all the dry ingredients, except the bran, in a large bowl. Then add the bran and stir to combine.

3. Add the goodies to the dry ingredients and toss to coat. If necessary, use your hands to coat the gooey bits.

4. Whisk the wet ingredients in a medium bowl or blend in a food processor. Pour the wet ingredients into the dry mixture. Stir just until mixed. *Do not overstir.*

5. Spoon the batter into a greased or papered muffin tin. Fill each cup nearly to the top.

6. Bake for 15 to 20 minutes.

7. Cool the muffins at least 10 minutes before removing from the tin.

YIELD
12–14
MUFFINS

DRY INGREDIENTS

2 cups unbleached white flour

1 cup whole wheat pastry flour

1/4 cup light brown sugar

2 teaspoons baking powder

1 teaspoon baking soda

1/4 teaspoon sea salt

WET INGREDIENTS

1 1/2 cups milk

1/2 cup honey

1/4 cup canola oil

1 large egg

1 1/2 teaspoons vanilla extract

GOODIES

1 cup coarsely chopped pecans

TOPPING

1/4 cup margarine or butter, melted

1/2 cup apple juice concentrate

1/4 cup light brown sugar

1 1/2 teaspoons cornstarch

1 large egg

1/2 cup coarsely chopped roasted pecans

1/4 teaspoon vanilla extract

Easy-Living Southern Pecan Muffins

I've taken my favorite pecan pie recipe and turned it into these unbeatable muffins. The thick, soft Southern pecan topping oozes into the cake below. Way to go, Dixie! Slice these muffins, fan them on a plate, and top with vanilla ice cream.

1. To prepare the topping, blend the margarine, apple juice concentrate, brown sugar, cornstarch, and egg in a food processor. Transfer the mixture to a small saucepan, place over medium heat, and stir until it thickens to a gravy-like consistency. Remove from the heat, add the pecans and vanilla, and stir to combine. Cool to room temperature.

2. Preheat the oven to 400°F.

3. Sift all the dry ingredients together in a large bowl. Add the goodies and toss to coat.

4. Whisk the wet ingredients in a medium bowl or blend in a food processor. Pour the wet ingredients into the dry mixture. Stir just until mixed. *Do not overstir.*

5. Spoon the batter into a greased or papered muffin tin. Fill each cup only about 2/3 full. Add the topping, taking care to spread it evenly over each cup. Too much topping piled high in the middle will prevent the muffins from rising properly.

6. Bake for 15 to 20 minutes.

7. Cool the muffins at least 10 minutes before removing from the tin.

Fruitcake Muffins

**YIELD
12–14
MUFFINS**

One Christmas, I decided to make fruitcakes for everyone I know. I painted small tins in holiday colors and bought Santa stickers to decorate them. But when I started to buy the ingredients, I realized I couldn't afford everything I needed. Fruitcakes are expensive! Not wanting to give up the idea, I converted my favorite fruitcake recipe to these Fruitcake Muffins. They're much less expensive and more satisfying than fruitcake. Use any combination of dried fruit and nuts you'd like.

1. Preheat the oven to 400°F.

2. Sift the dry ingredients together in a large bowl.

3. Whisk the wet ingredients in a medium bowl or blend in a food processor. Add the goodies and stir to combine. (The mixture will be fairly thicker.)

4. Pour the wet mixture into the dry ingredients. Stir just until mixed. *Do not overstir.*

5. Spoon the batter into a greased or papered muffin tin. Fill each cup nearly to the top.

6. Bake for 15 to 20 minutes.

7. Cool the muffins at least 10 minutes before removing from the tin.

DRY INGREDIENTS

1 cup whole wheat flour

1 cup unbleached white flour

1 1/2 teaspoons baking powder

1 1/2 teaspoons ground cinnamon

3/4 teaspoon ground ginger

1/2 teaspoon baking soda

1/2 teaspoon ground cloves

1/4 teaspoon sea salt

WET INGREDIENTS

2 ripe bananas, mashed (1 cup)

1/2 cup milk

1/4 cup canola oil

1/4 cup honey

1/4 cup molasses

2 large eggs

2 tablespoons grated orange peel

2 teaspoons vanilla extract

2 teaspoons brandy extract

GOODIES

1 1/2 cups coarsely chopped mixed dried fruit

1 1/2 cups coarsely chopped roasted nuts and/or seeds

YIELD
10–12
MUFFINS

Lyman's Chocolate Cheesecake Muffins

**YIELD
10–12
MUFFINS**

DRY INGREDIENTS

2 1/2 cups whole wheat pastry flour

1/2 cup light brown sugar

1/2 cup cocoa powder

2 teaspoons baking powder

I teaspoon baking soda

1/4 teaspoon sea salt

WET INGREDIENTS

8 ounces cream cheese, softened

1 1/4 cups milk

1/2 cup sour cream

I large egg

2 teaspoons vanilla extract

GOODIES

1 1/4 cups mini semi-sweet chocolate chips

My friend Lyman makes a chocolate cheesecake that knocks my socks off! I believe I've done justice to it with these muffins. Although I prefer using regular semi-sweet chocolate, use whatever type you prefer, including naturally sweetened chocolate chips (made with barley malt instead of sugar) or carob chips. To serve these muffins, I usually cut them into four or five slices, fan them on a plate, and top with fresh bing cherries or sliced strawberries.

1. Preheat the oven to 400°F.

2. Sift the dry ingredients together in a large bowl. Add the goodies and stir to combine.

3. Using the purée blade of a food processor, cream the cream cheese and sour cream. Add the remaining wet ingredients and blend. (If you do not have a food processor, use a hand-held mixer at medium speed.)

4. Pour the wet ingredients into the dry mixture. Stir just until mixed. *Do not overstir.*

5. Spoon the batter into a greased or papered muffin tin. Fill each cup nearly to the top.

6. Bake for 15 to 20 minutes.

7. Cool the muffins at least 10 minutes before removing from the tin.

Mocha Chip Muffins

When I lived in Virginia Beach, I often biked over to High's Ice Cream Parlor with my friends Jake and Lila. I usually ordered a chocolate shake blended with a teaspoon of instant coffee. The coffee granules dissolved, turning the rich chocolate flavor into a mocha delight. The three of us hummed all the way home. Well, I'm humming again over these muffins, which are flavorfully reminiscent of that shake. I like to crown them with Vanilla Cream Cheese Icing or Coffee Icing (page 193).

DRY INGREDIENTS

1 ½ cups whole wheat
pastry flour

1 cup whole wheat flour

½ cup light brown sugar

1 tablespoon baking
powder

¼ teaspoon sea salt

WET INGREDIENTS

1 ½ cups triple-strength
coffee, cooled

¼ cup canola oil

¼ cup butter or margarine,
melted

1 large egg

2 teaspoons vanilla
extract

GOODIES

¾ cup mini semi-sweet
chocolate chips

¾ cup coarsely chopped
roasted walnuts

1. Preheat the oven to 400°F.

2. Sift the dry ingredients together in a large bowl. Add the goodies and stir to combine.

3. Whisk the wet ingredients in a medium bowl or blend in a food processor. Pour the wet ingredients into the dry mixture. Stir just until mixed. *Do not overstir.*

4. Spoon the batter into a greased or papered muffin tin. Fill each cup nearly to the top.

5. Bake for 15 to 20 minutes.

6. Cool the muffins at least 10 minutes before removing from the tin.

YIELD
12
MUFFINS

Mincemeat Muffins

**YIELD
12
MUFFINS**

DRY INGREDIENTS

1 1/2 cups whole wheat pastry flour

1/2 cup unbleached white flour

1/2 cup brown rice flour

2 teaspoons baking powder

1 teaspoon baking soda

1/4 teaspoon sea salt

WET INGREDIENTS

1 1/4 cups buttermilk

1/4 cup apple juice concentrate

1/4 cup canola oil

1 large egg

1 teaspoon vanilla extract

1 teaspoon rum extract

GOODIES

2 cups mincemeat

In my family, mincemeat is a favorite treat during the holidays. Most holidays, my sister Betty makes her famous mincemeat chiffon pie and everyone goes bananas. I just had to make a mincemeat muffin. Use your favorite brand of mincemeat or make your own. Years ago, I came up with my own recipe and I am glad I did. It is so much better than any I have tasted. Why not do the same? If the mincemeat you use is very moist, use less buttermilk in this recipe.

1. Preheat the oven to 375°F.

2. Sift the dry ingredients together in a large bowl.

3. Whisk the wet ingredients in a medium bowl or blend in a food processor. Add the goodies and stir to combine.

4. Pour the wet mixture into the dry ingredients. Stir just until mixed. *Do not overstir.*

5. Spoon the batter into a greased or papered muffin tin. Fill each cup nearly to the top.

6. Bake for 15 to 20 minutes.

7. Cool the muffins at least 10 minutes before removing from the tin.

Old Fashioned Ginger-Currant Muffins

When I was young, my mom often packed gingersnaps with cream cheese in my school lunch pail. What a treat! Years later, I found myself in a quaint tea shop just outside London, savoring ginger tea cakes topped with currants and clotted cream. It took some time to create a muffin that captured those flavors and made me feel like that happy schoolgirl and contented English traveler again . . . but I did it. Try these muffins with lemon jelly, lemon curd, or Lemony Lemon Spread (page 190).

1. Preheat the oven to 400°F.

2. Sift the dry ingredients together in a large bowl.

3. Whisk the wet ingredients in a medium bowl or blend in a food processor. Add the goodies and stir to combine.

4. Pour the wet mixture into the dry ingredients. Stir just until mixed. *Do not overstir.*

5. Spoon the batter into a greased or papered muffin tin. Fill each cup nearly to the top.

6. Bake for 15 to 20 minutes.

7. Cool the muffins at least 10 minutes before removing from the tin.

YIELD 12 MUFFINS

DRY INGREDIENTS

1 cup whole wheat flour

1 cup unbleached white flour

1/2 cup brown rice flour

2 teaspoons baking powder

1 teaspoon baking soda

1 teaspoon ground cinnamon

1/2 teaspoon ground nutmeg

1/4 teaspoon sea salt

WET INGREDIENTS

1 cup buttermilk

1/2 cup apple juice concentrate

1/2 cup molasses

1/4 cup canola oil

1 large egg

1 tablespoon grated orange peel

GOODIES

2 tablespoons finely chopped fresh ginger root, or 1 tablespoon ground

1 1/2 cups currants

Orange-Chocolate Muffins

**YIELD
10–12
MUFFINS**

DRY INGREDIENTS

1 ¼ cups whole wheat flour

1 ¼ cups unbleached white flour

¼ cup light brown sugar

1 ½ teaspoons baking soda

1 teaspoon baking powder

¼ teaspoon sea salt

WET INGREDIENTS

1 ½ cups milk

½ cup honey

¼ cup canola oil

1 large egg

3 tablespoons grated orange peel

1 ½ teaspoons vanilla extract

GOODIES

¾ cup mini semi-sweet chocolate chips

These muffins were inspired by the orange-flavored reception sticks that my friends Steven and Randy always offer after one of their fabulous dinner parties. These thin sticks of hard candy have been hand-dipped in dark chocolate and are usually served with after-dinner coffee.

1. Preheat the oven to 375°F.

2. Sift the dry ingredients together in a large bowl. Add the goodies and stir to combine.

3. Whisk the wet ingredients in a medium bowl or blend in a food processor. Pour the wet ingredients into the dry mixture. Stir just until mixed. *Do not overstir.*

4. Spoon the batter into a greased or papered muffin tin. Fill each cup nearly to the top.

5. Bake for 15 to 20 minutes.

6. Cool the muffins at least 10 minutes before removing from the tin.

Patty's Reincarnated Cappuccino Muffins

YIELD
10–12
MUFFINS

My friend Patty has single handedly consumed dozens of my capuccino muffins over the past few years. It was only fitting that I named this new version for her. To help insure this recipe's success, use brewed coffee made with freshly ground coffee beans; add the honey while the coffee is hot; and blend the wet ingredients very well (or you may end up with little white clumps of unblended sour cream throughout the muffins).

1. Preheat the oven to 400°F.

2. Sift the dry ingredients together in a large bowl.

3. Whisk the wet ingredients in a medium bowl or blend in a food processor. Pour the wet ingredients into the dry ingredients. Stir just until mixed. *Do not overstir.*

4. Spoon the batter into a greased or papered muffin tin. Fill each cup nearly to the top.

5. Bake for 15 to 20 minutes.

6. Cool the muffins at least 10 minutes before removing from the tin.

DRY INGREDIENTS

1 1/2 cups unbleached white flour

1 cup whole wheat flour

1/2 cup light brown sugar

1 1/2 teaspoons baking soda

1 teaspoon baking powder

3 tablespoons cocoa powder

1 teaspoon ground cinnamon

1/4 teaspoon sea salt

WET INGREDIENTS

1 cup triple-strength coffee, cooled

3/4 cup sour cream

1/2 cup honey

1 large egg

1 teaspoon vanilla extract

Pistachio and Dried Cranberry Muffins

DRY INGREDIENTS

1 ³/₄ cups unbleached white flour

1 cup whole wheat flour

¹/₄ cup sugar

1 ¹/₂ teaspoons baking powder

1 teaspoon baking soda

¹/₄ teaspoon sea salt

WET INGREDIENTS

1 cup milk

¹/₄ cup apple juice concentrate

¹/₂ cup sour cream

¹/₂ cup honey

1 large egg

1 teaspoon vanilla extract

1 teaspoon grated orange peel

GOODIES

³/₄ cup dried cranberries

³/₄ cup chopped roasted pistachios

While buying nuts for this recipe at a local store, I found only pistachios that were still in their shells. I asked the clerk if she had any that were shelled. She replied, "Those are shelled." I said, "No. I mean the kind that have no shells." She said, "Oh. You mean unshelled, and we don't carry them." I was paralyzed. Had I been saying it wrong all these years? Shelled pistachios have had their shells removed. Right? I paid for the nuts, then went home and looked it up. Guess which expression is correct.

1. Preheat the oven to 400°F.

2. Sift the dry ingredients together in a large bowl.

3. Whisk the wet ingredients in a medium bowl or blend gently in a food processor. Add the goodies and stir to combine.

4. Pour the wet mixture into the dry ingredients. Stir just until mixed. *Do not overstir.*

5. Spoon the batter into a greased or papered muffin tin. Fill each cup nearly to the top.

6. Bake for 15 to 20 minutes.

7. Cool the muffins at least 10 minutes before removing from the tin.

Pumpkin-Chocolate Chip Muffins

**YIELD
12
MUFFINS**

It seems that I'm always looking for new and interesting ways to prepare pumpkin. I have found these to be great muffins to serve during the holidays or on special occasions. I use canned pumpkin purée in this recipe—mostly because it is always available and easy to use. You can also use sweet potato purée instead of pumpkin.

1. Preheat the oven to 400°F.

2. Sift the dry ingredients together in a large bowl. Add the goodies and stir to combine.

3. Whisk the wet ingredients in a medium bowl or blend in a food processor. Pour the wet ingredients into the dry mixture. Stir just until mixed. *Do not overstir.*

4. Spoon the batter into a greased or papered muffin tin. Fill each cup nearly to the top.

5. Bake for 15 to 20 minutes.

6. Cool the muffins at least 10 minutes before removing from the tin.

DRY INGREDIENTS

1 1/2 cups unbleached white flour

1 cup whole wheat flour

3/4 cup light brown sugar

1 1/2 teaspoons baking powder

1 teaspoon baking soda

1 1/2 teaspoons ground cinnamon

1/2 teaspoon ground nutmeg

1/2 teaspoon ground allspice

1/4 teaspoon ground cloves

1/4 teaspoon sea salt

WET INGREDIENTS

1 cup pumpkin purée

1 cup milk

1 large egg

1 teaspoon vanilla extract

GOODIES

1/2 cup mini semi-sweet chocolate chips

1/2 cup chopped roasted walnuts

YIELD
12
MUFFINS

DRY INGREDIENTS

1 1/2 cups unbleached white flour

3/4 cup whole wheat flour

3/4 cup light brown sugar

2 teaspoons baking powder

1 teaspoon baking soda

2 teaspoons ground cinnamon

1 teaspoon ground nutmeg

1/4 teaspoon sea salt

WET INGREDIENTS

1 cup pumpkin purée

1 cup milk

1/4 cup canola oil

1 tablespoon molasses, warmed

1 large egg

GOODIES

1 cup roasted pumpkin seeds

3/4 cup raisins

Pumpkin-Pumpkin Seed Muffins

Pumpkin seeds often get separated from the pumpkin and are thrown out. What a shame—pumpkin pulp and pumpkin seeds go well together; they were born that way. With these muffins, I've put the seeds back in the pumpkin and added a few goodies to boot. For a nice holiday treat, place a basketful of mini Pumpkin-Pumpkin Seed Muffins on your dinner table between the steamed broccoli and the cranberry sauce. It will look like a bouquet of fall flowers.

1. Preheat the oven to 400°F.

2. Sift the dry ingredients together in a large bowl.

3. Whisk the wet ingredients in a medium bowl or blend in a food processor. Add the goodies and stir to combine.

4. Pour the wet mixture into the dry ingredients. Stir just until mixed. *Do not overstir.*

5. Spoon the batter into a greased or papered muffin tin. Fill each cup nearly to the top.

6. Bake for 15 to 20.

7. Cool the muffins at least 10 minutes before removing from the tin.

Roger's Chocolate Fruit & Nut Muffins

YIELD
12
MUFFINS

These muffins were made for my nephew Roger, who recommended the ingredient combination after eating a Cadbury chocolate bar with fruit and nuts. As an added treat, try them with Chocolate-Peanut Butter Spread (page 189).

1. Preheat the oven to 400°F.

2. Sift the dry ingredients together in a large bowl.

3. Whisk the wet ingredients in a medium bowl or blend in a food processor. Add the goodies and stir to combine.

4. Pour the wet mixture into the dry ingredients. Stir just until mixed. *Do not overstir.*

5. Spoon the batter into a greased or papered muffin tin. Fill each cup nearly to the top.

6. Bake for 15 to 20 minutes.

7. Cool the muffins at least 10 minutes before removing from the tin.

DRY INGREDIENTS

1 1/2 cups whole wheat flour

1 cup unbleached white flour

1/2 cup light brown sugar

6 tablespoons cocoa powder

2 teaspoons baking powder

1/4 teaspoon sea salt

WET INGREDIENTS

1 1/2 cups milk

1/2 cup sour cream

1/4 cup chocolate syrup

1 tablespoon canola oil

1 large egg

2 teaspoons vanilla extract

1 teaspoon grated orange peel

GOODIES

3/4 cup raisins

3/4 cup chopped roasted walnuts

Rum Raisin Muffins

YIELD
10–12
MUFFINS

DRY INGREDIENTS

1 1/2 cups whole wheat flour

3/4 cups unbleached white flour

1/2 cup light brown sugar

1 3/4 teaspoons baking soda

1/2 teaspoon baking powder

1 teaspoon ground nutmeg

1/4 teaspoon ground cardamom

1/4 teaspoon sea salt

WET INGREDIENTS

1 cup vanilla yogurt

3/4 cup water

1/2 cup applesauce

1/4 cup canola oil

1 large egg

2 1/2 teaspoons rum flavoring

1 1/2 teaspoons grated lemon peel

1 teaspoon vanilla extract

GOODIES

1 cup golden raisins

Made with the fabulous flavors of eggnog, these muffins can accompany any holiday meal. Along with a cup of Earl Grey tea, they are a great way to start the day. As a lunchtime dessert, top them with a scoop of rum raisin or French vanilla ice cream. And at holiday banquets, serve them alongside the turkey or ham. You may note that I've used rum extract rather than the real thing. Alcohol puts a damper on muffins. It reacts in funny ways with the rising agents and makes them go flat.

1. Preheat the oven to 375°F.

2. Sift the dry ingredients together in a large bowl.

3. Whisk the wet ingredients in a medium bowl or blend in a food processor. Add the goodies and stir to combine.

4. Pour the wet mixture into the dry ingredients. Stir just until mixed. *Do not overstir.*

5. Spoon the batter into a greased or papered muffin tin. Fill each cup nearly to the top.

6. Bake for 15 to 20 minutes.

7. Cool the muffins at least 10 minutes before removing from the tin.

Sugar Plum Fairy Muffins

**YIELD
10–12
MUFFINS**

Here's a muffin that matches the lightness and agility of the Nutcracker's dance of the sugar plum fairies. The combination of sour cream, applesauce, orange peel, and lemon peel gives this muffin its light and fruity appeal. Plum preserves and crystal sugar make the perfect topper; but if you can't find plum preserves, plain old grape jam (not jelly) works too.

DRY INGREDIENTS

1 1/4 cups whole wheat flour

3/4 cup unbleached white flour

1/2 cup brown rice flour

1/4 cup sugar

1 1/4 teaspoons baking soda

1 teaspoon baking powder

1/4 teaspoon sea salt

1. To prepare the glaze topping, combine the water and cornstarch in a small saucepan and stir to dissolve any lumps. Add the plum preserves and stir the mixture over medium-high heat about 3 minutes, or until it thickens. Remove from heat and cool to room temperature.

2. Preheat the oven to 375°F.

3. Sift the dry ingredients together in a large bowl.

4. Whisk the wet ingredients in a medium bowl or blend in a food processor. Pour the wet ingredients into the dry ingredients. Stir just until mixed. *Do not overstir.*

5. Spoon the batter into a greased or papered muffin tin. Fill each cup nearly to the top.

6. Bake for 15 to 20 minutes.

7. Cool the muffins 10 minutes.

8. Spoon a teaspoon of the glaze evenly over the top of each muffin. Sprinkle with a large pinch of pearl sugar. The topping will harden a little as it continues to cool. Cool the muffins another 10 minutes before removing from the tin.

WET INGREDIENTS

1 cup milk

3/4 cup applesauce

3/4 cup sour cream

1 large egg

2 teaspoon grated lemon peel

1 1/2 teaspoons grated orange peel

1 teaspoon vanilla extract

GLAZE TOPPING

1/4 cup water

1 1/2 teaspoons cornstarch

1/4 cup plum preserves

2 tablespoons pearl sugar crystals

White Chocolate with Raspberries Muffins

**YIELD
12
MUFFINS**

DRY INGREDIENTS

1 cup whole wheat
pastry flour

1 cup unbleached
white flour

$\frac{1}{2}$ cup whole wheat flour

$\frac{3}{4}$ cup sugar

1 $\frac{1}{2}$ teaspoons baking
powder

1 teaspoon baking
soda

$\frac{1}{4}$ teaspoon sea salt

WET INGREDIENTS

1 $\frac{1}{2}$ cups milk

$\frac{1}{2}$ cup sour cream

1 large egg

1 tablespoon vanilla
extract

GOODIES

$\frac{3}{4}$ cup firm fresh raspberries,
washed, patted dry,
and halved

$\frac{3}{4}$ cup coarsely chopped
white chocolate

I'll never forget the first time I tasted these muffins. I had made them to enjoy with some friends. Heads hung over our plates, we bit into them, still-warm-from-the-oven. There was a prolonged pause, then a simultaneous "Oh, my God!" It makes no difference if you use chunks or chips in this recipe, just be sure to chop them to a coarse powder. This allows the chocolate to melt into the muffin and spread its delicious goodness throughout. Also try them with chopped hazelnuts instead of raspberries.

1. Preheat the oven to 400°F.

2. Sift the dry ingredients together in a large bowl. Add the goodies and toss to coat. (This will keep the raspberries from bleeding into the rest of the batter.)

3. Whisk the wet ingredients in a medium bowl or blend in a food processor. Pour the wet ingredients into the dry mixture. Stir just until mixed, taking care not to break the raspberries. *Do not overstir.*

4. Spoon the batter into a greased or papered muffin tin. Fill each cup nearly to the top.

5. Bake for 15 to 20 minutes.

6. Cool the muffins at least 15 to 20 minutes before removing from the tin.

6. Extra-Effort-But-Worth-It Muffins

Learn to labor and to wait.

—HENRY WADSWORTH LONGFELLOW, *A PSALM OF LIFE*

My main criteria for making muffins has always been the following: They must be nutritious and quick and easy to bake. Given our busy schedules and the many excuses we seem to make for not eating right, I want to be sure that we could at least optimize the frequency and quality of our muffin consumption. But then as I baked and baked, and as new ideas for muffins popped into my head, I found that sometimes I wanted to extend myself a bit and spend more time with the creative process. Besides, we're not *always* in a hurry, are we?

In this chapter, you'll find lots of scrumptious muffins that require a little more of your effort and attention. So what's this extra effort I'm talking about? In some muffins, it involves filling the bottoms of the cups with interesting treats so that the muffins are best displayed (and enjoyed!) upside-down. These include such recipes as my Cinnamon Sticky Muffins, Flipped Apple Muffins, and Pineapple Upside-Down

Muffins. For other recipes, like the Gingerbread Muffins with Lemon Curd Filling and my Jim Dandy Jelly Crumb Muffins, the extra effort means adding a surprise filling in each muffin, so your friends and family will enjoy an added treat with each bite. For still other recipes, such as the Devil's Food Muffins with Vanilla Cream Cheese Icing and my Marvelous Marble Muffins with Coffee Icing, the extra effort involves crowning the muffins with a luscious frosting. You get the picture.

No matter which muffins you choose, no matter how much effort they require, I think you'll agree that they are worth it! Enjoy!

Flipped Apple Muffins

YIELD
12
MUFFINS

The juicy "topping" permeates these unbelievably moist muffins as they bake. When removed from the oven and flipped upside down, they are further soaked with juice. Chopped apples crown the tops for an impressive presentation. Because the topping may boil during baking, place a tray beneath the tin to catch the overflow (and spare your oven).

DRY INGREDIENTS

1 cup whole wheat flour

1 cup unbleached white flour

1 1/2 teaspoons baking soda

1 teaspoon baking powder

1 teaspoon ground cinnamon

1/4 teaspoon sea salt

1 cup oat bran

WET INGREDIENTS

1 cup milk

1/2 cup applesauce

1/2 cup honey

1 large egg

2 teaspoons grated lemon peel

1 teaspoon vanilla extract

FLIPPED "TOPPING"

1 tablespoon light margarine

1/2 cup light brown sugar

1/2 cup apple juice

3 small apples, chopped (do not grate)

2 teaspoons rum flavoring

1. Preheat the oven to 375°F.

2. To prepare the topping, melt the margarine in a small saucepan over medium heat. Add the sugar and cook, stirring constantly for 5 minutes, or until it begins to brown. Add the apple juice and apples, and cook 5 minutes more. Remove from heat and stir in the rum flavoring. Spoon the mixture into a greased muffin tin, dividing it evenly among the cups. (It should measure a little less than 1 tablespoon per cup.) Set the prepared tin aside.

3. Sift together all the dry ingredients, except the bran, in a large bowl. Then add the bran and stir to combine.

4. Whisk the wet ingredients in a medium bowl or blend in a food processor. Pour the wet ingredients into the dry ingredients. Stir just until mixed. *Do not overstir.*

5. Spoon the batter into the prepared muffin tin. Fill each cup nearly to the top.

6. Bake for 15 to 20 minutes.

7. When the muffins are done, immediately turn them upside-down on a platter or baking sheet. *Do not remove the muffin tin.* Cool at least 10 minutes before removing the tin. You may need a knife to help free the muffins.

YIELD
12
MUFFINS

DRY INGREDIENTS

1 ½ cups whole wheat flour

1 cup unbleached white flour

½ cup light brown sugar

1 ½ teaspoons baking soda

1 teaspoon baking powder

1 ½ tablespoons ground ginger

1 ½ teaspoons ground cinnamon

1 teaspoon ground nutmeg

¼ teaspoon salt

WET INGREDIENTS

1 ½ cups buttermilk

½ cup molasses

¼ cup canola oil

1 large egg

1 ½ tablespoons grated orange peel

1 ½ tablespoons finely chopped fresh ginger root

GOODIES

¾ cup lemon curd

Gingerbread Muffins with Lemon Curd Filling

If you've ever spread lemon curd—a popular English dessert filling—on gingerbread, you'll know why I created these muffins. Like peanut butter and toast, lemon curd and gingerbread were made for each other. You can find lemon curd in the imported food aisle or the jam and jelly section of most large grocery stores. I have even seen it stocked with the pie fillings and cake ingredients.

1. Preheat the oven to 400°F.

2. Sift the dry ingredients together in a large bowl.

3. Whisk the wet ingredients in a medium bowl or blend in a food processor. Pour the wet ingredients into the dry ingredients. Stir just until mixed. *Do not overstir.*

4. Spoon the batter into a greased or papered muffin tin. Fill each cup nearly to the top.

5. Bake for 15 to 20 minutes.

6. Cool the muffins at least 10 minutes before removing from the tin. When the muffins have cooled to room temperature, squeeze about a tablespoon of lemon curd into each, using a pastry tube.

Glazed Ginger-Carrot Muffins

I love glazed carrots. I lightly steam carrot slices with grated ginger and then top them with honey and butter just before serving. People always want to know what magic I performed. "Just ginger and honey," I reply. "Just ginger and honey." I've recreated this fabulous ingredient combination in these muffins, which make a scrumptious dessert! They're best served warm— fresh from the oven or reheated.

1. Preheat the oven to 400°F.

2. Sift the dry ingredients together in a large bowl.

3. Whisk the wet ingredients in a medium bowl or blend in a food processor. Add the goodies and stir to combine.

4. Pour the wet mixture into the dry ingredients. Stir just until mixed. *Do not overstir.*

5. Spoon the batter into a greased or papered muffin tin. Fill each cup nearly to the top.

6. Bake for 15 to 20 minutes.

7. While the muffins bake, prepare the glaze topping.

8. Cool the muffins at least 10 minutes before removing from the tin. Glaze the tops and cool an additional 10 minutes before digging in.

YIELD
12 MUFFINS

DRY INGREDIENTS
$1\frac{1}{4}$ cup whole wheat pastry flour

1 cup whole wheat flour

$\frac{1}{2}$ cup brown rice flour

2 teaspoons baking powder

1 teaspoon baking soda

$\frac{1}{4}$ teaspoon sea salt

WET INGREDIENTS
$1\frac{3}{4}$ cups milk

$\frac{1}{4}$ cup canola oil

1 large egg

1 tablespoon grated orange peel

GOODIES
1 cup grated carrots

$1\frac{1}{2}$ tablespoons finely chopped fresh ginger root, or $\frac{3}{4}$ tablespoon powder

TOPPING
Orange Glaze (page 191)

Cinnamon Sticky Muffins

YIELD
12 STANDARD OR
6 JUMBO MUFFINS

DRY INGREDIENTS

1 ½ cups whole wheat pastry flour

1 cup whole wheat flour

½ cup unbleached white flour

1 tablespoon baking powder

2 teaspoons ground cinnamon

¼ teaspoon sea salt

WET INGREDIENTS

1 cup applesauce

1 cup milk

¼ cup canola oil

1 large egg

1 teaspoon vanilla extract

GOODIES

1 cup coarsely chopped roasted walnuts

1 cup coarsely chopped roasted sunflower seeds

12 heaping teaspoons margarine or butter

12 heaping teaspoons light brown sugar

My Cinnamon Sticky Muffins are moist, cakey, and covered with nuts. They are impossible to resist. Try this recipe with jumbo muffin tins instead of the standard 3-inch ones, and try to serve them warm from the oven or reheated. Sliced apples or pears and a cup of spice tea are great accompaniments.

1. Preheat the oven to 375°F.

2. Sift the dry ingredients together in a large bowl.

3. Combine the walnuts and sunflower seeds in a small bowl. Add 1 cup of this mixture to the dry ingredients and stir to combine. Reserve the remaining mixture for the topping (see Step 4).

4. To prepare the muffin tins, place 1 heaping teaspoon of margarine into each cup, followed by 1 heaping teaspoon of brown sugar, and 2 heaping teaspoons of the reserved walnut-sunflower seed mixture. (If using jumbo muffin tins, double these amounts.)

5. Whisk the wet ingredients in a medium bowl or blend in a food processor. Pour the wet ingredients into the dry mixture. Stir just until mixed. *Do not overstir.*

6. Spoon the batter into the muffin tins. Fill each cup nearly to the top.

7. Bake 15 to 20 minutes for standard muffins, 20 to 25 minutes for jumbo.

8. When the muffins are done, immediately turn them upside-down on a platter or baking sheet. *Do not remove the muffin tin.* Cool at least 10 minutes before removing the tin. You may need a knife to help free the muffins.

Charity Nut Muffins

YIELD
12
MUFFINS

Charity nut cups are little pies made in mini-muffin tins. The tins are lined with pie crust and filled with a delightful blend of nuts, brown sugar, and butter. Mmm. Mmm. Mmm! The nutty, crunchy filling makes them so appealing. I've transformed this wonderful holiday dessert into an equally delightful muffin. For added nutrition, I've laced the nut filling with toasted wheat germ. Enjoy them with your favorite apple butter. They'll knock your socks off!

1. Preheat the oven to 400°F.

2. Sift the dry ingredients together in a large bowl.

3. Combine the walnuts, wheat germ, and brown sugar in a small bowl. Reserve 1 cup of this goodie mixture to use as a topping (see Step 6), and add the remaining mixture to the dry ingredients. Stir to combine.

4. Combine the softened margarine with the reserved goodie mixture to form a crumbly topping. Set aside.

5. Whisk the wet ingredients in a medium bowl or blend in a food processor. Pour the wet ingredients into the dry mixture. Stir just until mixed. *Do not overstir.*

6. Spoon the batter into a greased or papered muffin tin, filling each cup only about $2/3$ full to leave room for the topping. Top each cup of batter with a generous amount of the topping mixture (use it all), taking care to sprinkle it evenly over each cup. Too much topping piled high in the middle will prevent the muffins from rising properly.

7. Bake for 15 to 20 minutes.

8. Cool the muffins at least 10 minutes before removing from the tin.

DRY INGREDIENTS

$1^3/_4$ cups whole wheat pastry flour

$1/_2$ cup whole wheat flour

$1/_2$ cup unbleached white flour

1 tablespoon soy flour

2 teaspoons baking powder

1 teaspoon baking soda

$1/_4$ teaspoon sea salt

WET INGREDIENTS

1 cup buttermilk

$1/_2$ cup water

$1/_2$ cup honey

$1/_4$ cup canola oil

1 large egg

1 teaspoon vanilla extract

GOODIES

$1^1/_4$ cups finely chopped roasted walnuts

$1/_2$ cup toasted wheat germ

$1/_2$ cup light brown sugar

$1/_4$ cup margarine or butter, softened to room temperature

Devil's Food Muffins with Vanilla Cream Cheese Icing

DRY INGREDIENTS

1 ½ cups unbleached white flour

¾ cup whole wheat flour

¾ cup sugar

6 tablespoons cocoa powder

1 ½ teaspoons baking powder

1 teaspoon baking soda

¼ teaspoon sea salt

WET INGREDIENTS

1 ½ cups buttermilk

½ cup chocolate syrup

1 large egg

1 ½ teaspoons vanilla extract

GOODIES

¾ cup mini semi-sweet chocolate chips

TOPPING

Vanilla Cream Cheese Icing (page 193)

The way I see it, chocolate is one of life's essentials. There's food, clothing, shelter, and chocolate. Right? So how is it that we've come to associate chocolate with sin and guilt and overindulgence, while white cake is for angels? I think terms like "death-by-chocolate" and "devil's food" have placed chocolate in the wrong light and make us feel wicked. I suggest that you thoroughly enjoy these muffins without feeling devilish or wicked—unless, of course, you want to.

1. Preheat the oven to 400°F.

2. Sift the dry ingredients together in a large bowl. Add the goodies and toss to coat.

3. Whisk the wet ingredients together in a medium bowl or blend in a food processor. Pour the wet ingredients into the dry mixture. Stir just until mixed. *Do not overstir.*

4. Spoon the batter into a greased or papered muffin tin. Fill each cup nearly to the top.

5. Bake for 15 to 20 minutes.

6. While the muffins bake, prepare the icing. Store in the refrigerator until ready to use.

7. Cool the muffins at least 10 minutes before removing from the tin. Allow them to further cool to room temperature before adding the icing.

Trust Your Own Experience

For me, the muffin-creating process goes something like this: I taste or read about or remember an interesting combination of flavors that I imagine would make a great muffin. Then I prepare a first draft of a recipe and test it. Sometimes I'm right on target and don't need to make changes in my subsequent test runs. But other times I'm way off.

When I made Catherine's Lemon-Red Raspberry Muffins (page 40) from my first-draft recipe, I followed the usual procedure. I sifted the dry ingredients, added and tossed the goodies, then blended the wet ingredients in my food processor. But as I was about to pour the wet ingredients into the dry mixture, I hesitated. There was a gentle force preventing me from doing so. My instinct told me there was too much liquid. If I used it all, the batter would be too runny and I would have to throw it out and start all over again. Or I would have to compensate for the excess liquid by adding more flour. Then, of course, I would have to stir the batter too much and my muffins would be rubbery and filled with holes.

For a few moments these thoughts ricocheted around the inner walls of my brain. You know how it can be when there are so many variables to con-

sider in the moments just before we act. One idea brings up a counter idea and this, in turn, often brings us back to our original impulse.

In the end, my "what-the-heck" reflex won out and I poured the wet ingredients into the dry ingredients.

The batter was too wet.

I had to add more flour, which caused me to stir the batter too much. And my muffins were rubbery and full of holes. Plus, the added stirring made the raspberries bleed into the batter so badly that the muffins turned an unappealing purplish color instead of the light lemon yellow I had envisioned. I ended up throwing out the whole batch.

It's the same with writing. After working on this book's Preface, I was just about ready to ask Rick, my writing partner, to read it. However, two sentences kept jumping off the page—they didn't seem right. I thought, "Ah, what the heck. It's probably just me. I'm being too fastidious. Rick will be more generous in his criticism." When Rick got back to me, he had flagged only two sentences. Yup. They were the two I had already flagged myself.

The mistakes I have made while creating muffin recipes are the same ones I've made in life. And

I think they are common human experiences. We don't always trust our own intuitive sense of what is right.

If, for one reason or another, you feel like making changes in my recipes, or if you go wild and decide to create muffin recipes of your own, do it! Trust your own sense of what is right and, if you are like me, over time you will notice a growing confidence in your own experience. And it will make you very happy.

Blueberry-Peach Schnapps Muffins

YIELD 11–12 MUFFINS

DRY INGREDIENTS

- $3/4$ cup whole wheat pastry flour
- $1/2$ cup whole wheat flour
- $1/2$ cup unbleached white flour
- $1/2$ cup sugar
- $1 1/2$ teaspoons baking soda
- 1 teaspoon baking powder
- $1/2$ teaspoon ground nutmeg
- $1/4$ teaspoon sea salt
- 1 cup oat or wheat bran

WET INGREDIENTS

- $3/4$ cup milk
- 1 large egg
- $1/2$ teaspoon lemon extract

One of the most felicitous acts of nature is the simultaneous ripening of peaches and blueberries. Individually their flavors stand out in a crowd, but in combination . . . what can I say? It's perfection! For this recipe, select small, firm blueberries, and use canned peaches packed in fruit juice. (Fresh peaches are too acidic.) Before adding the glaze, pull the muffins away from the sides of the cups, so the glaze can run down the sides and soak the entire muffin. Mmm.

1. Preheat the oven to 375°F.

2. Sift together all the dry ingredients, except the bran, in a large bowl. Then add the bran and stir to combine. Add the blueberries and toss to coat.

3. Purée the peaches in a food processor or blender to yield about $1 1/4$ cups purée. Add the wet ingredients and pulse to blend. (You can also use a fork or a potato ricer to mash the peaches, then blend in the wet ingredients by hand.)

4. Pour the wet mixture into the dry mixture. Stir just until mixed. *Do not overstir.* Spoon the batter into a greased or papered muffin tin. Fill each cup nearly to the top.

5. Bake for 15 to 20 minutes.

6. While the muffins bake, prepare the glaze. Melt the margarine in a small saucepan over medium heat. Add the sugar and cook, stirring constantly for 5 minutes, or until it begins to brown. Remove from the heat and stir in the schnapps.

7. After removing the muffins from the oven, immediately pierce the top of each six or seven times with a skewer or toothpick. Using all the glaze, drizzle it evenly over each muffin until completely absorbed.

8. Cool the muffins at least 10 minutes before removing from the tin.

GOODIES

³/₄ cup firm fresh blueberries, washed and patted dry

16-ounce can peaches packed in fruit juice, well drained

GLAZE

1 tablespoon light margarine

¹/₄ cup sugar

¹/₄ cup peach schnapps

Glazed Sunrise Blueberry Muffins

DRY INGREDIENTS

1 $\frac{1}{2}$ cups unbleached white flour

1 $\frac{1}{2}$ cups whole wheat pastry flour

2 teaspoons baking powder

1 teaspoon baking soda

$\frac{1}{4}$ teaspoon sea salt

WET INGREDIENTS

1 $\frac{3}{4}$ cups milk

$\frac{1}{2}$ cup honey

$\frac{1}{2}$ cup margarine or butter, melted

1 large egg

3 tablespoons grated lemon or orange peel (or both!)

GOODIES

1 $\frac{1}{4}$ cups firm fresh blueberries, washed and patted dry

TOPPING

Citrus Honey Glaze (page 192)

When I watch the sun come up, I'm reminded of a poem by Oliver Wendell Holmes:

> **The morning light, which rains its quivering beams**
> **Wide o'er the plains, the summits, and the streams,**
> **In one broad blaze expands its golden flow**
> **On all that answers to its glance below.**

I think these muffins are a great way to "answer the glance" of sunrise . . . and the glaze adds an extra burst of sunshine.

1. Preheat the oven to 375°F.

2. Sift the dry ingredients together in a large bowl. Add the goodies and toss to coat.

3. Whisk the wet ingredients in a medium bowl or blend in a food processor. Pour the wet ingredients into the dry mixture. Stir just until mixed. *Do not overstir.*

4. Spoon the batter into a greased or papered muffin tin. Fill each cup nearly to the top.

5. Bake for 15 to 20 minutes.

6. While the muffins bake, prepare the glaze topping.

7. Cool the muffins at least 10 minutes before removing from the tin. Glaze the tops, and cool an additional 10 minutes before digging in.

Grand Marnier Creamsicle Muffins

YIELD
12
MUFFINS

Whenever my computer's spell-checker sees the word "Marnier," it asks, "Do you mean 'mariner'?" Hmm. For a moment, I doubt my spelling. So for the third time, I get up to check the label on the bottle of Grand Marnier. Oh computers, how easily they can make us doubt what we know! I use Grand Marnier in this recipe, but you can use any orange-flavored liqueur. Your computer's spell-checker may have an easier time with it.

1. Preheat the oven to 375°F.

2. Sift the dry ingredients together in a large bowl.

3. Whisk the wet ingredients in a medium bowl or blend in a food processor. Pour the wet ingredients into the dry ingredients. Stir just until mixed. *Do not overstir.*

4. Spoon the batter into a greased or papered muffin tin. Fill each cup nearly to the top.

5. Bake for 15 to 20 minutes.

6. While the muffins bake, prepare the glaze. Melt the margarine in a small saucepan over medium heat. Add the sugar and cook, stirring constantly for 5 minutes, or until it begins to brown. Remove from the heat and stir in the Grand Marnier.

7. After removing the muffins from the oven, immediately pierce the top of each six or seven times with a skewer or toothpick. Drizzle the glaze evenly over each muffin. Cool at least 10 minutes before removing from the tin.

DRY INGREDIENTS

1 1/4 cups whole wheat flour

1 cup unbleached white flour

1/2 cup brown rice flour

1 1/2 teaspoons baking powder

1 teaspoon baking soda

1/4 teaspoon sea salt

WET INGREDIENTS

1 1/4 cup milk

1/2 cup sour cream

1/2 cup honey

1 large egg

2 tablespoons grated orange peel

1 1/2 teaspoons vanilla extract

GRAND MARNIER GLAZE

1 tablespoon margarine

1/4 cup sugar

1/4 cup Grand Marnier

Jim Dandy Jelly Crumb Muffins

Yield 11–12 Muffins

DRY INGREDIENTS

1 cup unbleached white flour
3/4 cup whole wheat flour
1/2 cup barley flour
1 teaspoon baking powder
1 teaspoon baking soda
1/4 teaspoon sea salt

WET INGREDIENTS

1 1/4 cups buttermilk
1/2 cup water
1/2 cup honey
1 large egg
2 teaspoons grated lemon peel
1 teaspoon vanilla extract

GOODIES

1/2 cup jelly, jam, or fruit preserves

CRUMBLE TOPPING

1/2 cup unbleached white flour
2 tablespoons light brown sugar
1/8 teaspoon ground cinnamon
2 tablespoons margarine, softened

"Jim Dandy: A person or thing that is excellent or first rate."
What I especially like about these Jim Dandy muffins is that you can fill them with any kind of jelly, jam, or preserves—and you can use a variety of fillings in each batch. You can, for example, use your favorite fruit preserves in two or three muffins, your partner's favorite filling in another few, your kid's in yet another two or three, and Aunt Tillie's favorite in what's left. You get the picture. It will seem as if you baked all day!

1. Preheat the oven to 375°F.

2. To prepare the crumble topping, combine the flour, brown sugar, and cinnamon in a medium bowl. Using a pastry blender or two knives, cut the margarine into the mixture to form crumbles. Set aside.

3. Sift the dry ingredients together in a large bowl.

4. Whisk the wet ingredients in a medium bowl or blend in a food processor. Pour the wet ingredients into the dry ingredients. Stir just until mixed. *Do not overstir.*

5. Spoon the batter into a greased or papered muffin tin. Fill each cup nearly to the top. Top each cup of batter with 2 teaspoons crumble topping, taking care to spread it evenly over each cup. Too much topping piled high in the middle will prevent the muffins from rising properly.

6. Bake for 15 to 20 minutes.

7. Cool the muffins at least 10 minutes before removing from the tin. When the muffins have cooled to room temperature, squeeze about a tablespoon of jelly into each, using a pastry tube.

Marvelous Marbled Muffins with Coffee Icing

Marbled breads and cakes are distinctive—very impressive. That's why I wanted to include a marbled muffin in this cookbook. I was so happy with both their appearance and flavor, I decided to top them with coffee-flavored cream cheese icing. (I love the combination of coffee and chocolate.) But feel free to use any cream cheese icing in Chapter 8, or skip the icing and serve these muffins sliced and topped with ice cream or frozen yogurt.

1. Preheat the oven to 400°F.

2. Sift the dry ingredients together in a large bowl, and then evenly divide the mixture into two separate bowls. Add the goodies to one of the bowls and stir to combine.

3. Whisk the wet ingredients in a medium bowl or blend in a food processor. Pour half the wet mixture into each bowl of dry ingredient. Stir just until mixed. *Do not overstir.*

4. In a greased or papered muffin tin, spoon one scoop of the chocolate batter and one scoop of vanilla batter into each cup. Use all the batter for 12 muffins. With a knife, gently swirl the batters in each cup to marbleize.

5. Bake for 15 to 20 minutes.

6. While the muffins bake, prepare the icing.

7. Cool the muffins at least 10 minutes before removing from the tin. Allow them to further cool to room temperature before adding the icing.

YIELD
12
MUFFINS

DRY INGREDIENTS
1 1/4 cups whole wheat flour

1 1/4 cups unbleached white flour

1 1/2 teaspoons baking soda

1 teaspoon baking powder

1/4 teaspoon sea salt

3/4 cup sugar

WET INGREDIENTS
1 1/2 cups buttermilk

1/2 cup water

2 large egg whites

3 teaspoons vanilla extract

GOODIES
3 tablespoons cocoa powder

1/4 cup coarsely chopped semi-sweet chocolate

TOPPING
Coffee Icing (page 193)

Pineapple Upside-Down Muffins

YIELD
12
MUFFINS

DRY INGREDIENTS

1 ½ cups whole wheat flour

1 cup whole wheat pastry flour

¼ cup light brown sugar

1 ½ teaspoon baking soda

1 teaspoon baking powder

¼ teaspoon sea salt

WET INGREDIENTS

1 cup applesauce

½ cup buttermilk

½ cup water

¼ cup pineapple juice

1 large egg

2 teaspoons grated lemon peel

1 teaspoon vanilla extract

"TOPPING"

¼ cup margarine, melted

¼ cup light brown sugar

8-ounce can crushed pineapple, well drained

Upside-down muffins are twice the fun of right-side-up muffins. First, there's the fun of creatively filling the bottom of each muffin cup with ingredients that will eventually be on top. Then there's the added kick of flipping the tin over and witnessing the results of your artistry. And here's a tip: When you drain the pineapple for the "topping," reserve the juice to use as part of the wet ingredients.

1. Preheat the oven to 375°F.

2. To create the "topping," spoon 1 teaspoon of margarine in each cup of a greased muffin tin. Top with 1 heaping teaspoon of brown sugar, distributing it evenly in the bottom of each cup. Add 1 heaping teaspoon of crushed pineapple, spreading it evenly over the brown sugar. Use all of the pineapple. Set aside.

3. Sift the dry ingredients together in a large bowl.

4. Whisk the wet ingredients in a medium bowl or blend in a food processor. Pour the wet ingredients into the dry ingredients. Stir just until mixed. *Do not overstir.*

5. Spoon the batter in the muffin tin over the "topping." Fill each cup nearly to the top.

6. Bake for 15 to 20 minutes.

7. When the muffins are done, immediately turn them upside-down on a platter or baking sheet. *Do not remove the muffin tin.* Cool at least 10 minutes before removing the tin. You may need a knife to help free the muffins.

Wantana's Thai Custard Muffins

YIELD
12
MUFFINS

I met Wantana, a slight Thai woman, during a retreat at a Buddhist monastery in England. Each Friday, she arrived to cook for those in attendance. One of her specialties was an out-of-this-world Thai custard, which prompted the creation of these muffins.

1. Preheat the oven to 400°F.

2. Sift the dry ingredients together in a large bowl.

3. Whisk the wet ingredients in a medium bowl or blend in a food processor. Pour the wet ingredients into the dry ingredients. Stir just until mixed. *Do not overstir.* Spoon the batter into a greased or papered muffin tin. Fill each cup nearly to the top.

4. Bake for 15 to 20 minutes.

5. While the muffins bake, prepare the custard sauce. Melt the margarine in a saucepan over medium heat. Add the cornstarch and stir to a smooth paste. Add the milk and brown sugar. Stirring frequently, cook the mixture over low heat about 15 minutes or until it thickens. Remove from the heat, add the vanilla, and stir to a smooth consistency. Set aside to cool.

6. Cool the muffins at least 10 minutes before removing from the tin.

7. When ready to serve, place each muffin in the center of a small serving dish. Top with approximately 1 tablespoon of custard sauce and a large pinch of coconut. Serve warm.

DRY INGREDIENTS

1 cup whole wheat pastry flour

1 cup unbleached white flour

$1/2$ cup whole wheat flour

$3/4$ cup light brown sugar

2 teaspoons baking powder

1 teaspoons baking soda

$1/4$ teaspoon sea salt

WET INGREDIENTS

1 $1/2$ cups coconut milk

$3/4$ cup sour cream

1 large egg

1 teaspoon vanilla extract

CUSTARD SAUCE

1 tablespoon light margarine

1 $1/2$ tablespoons cornstarch

$3/4$ cup milk

3 tablespoons light brown sugar

1 teaspoon vanilla extract

GOODIES

$1/2$ cup flaked coconut

Wheat Berry Surprise Muffins

**YIELD
16
MUFFINS**

DRY INGREDIENTS

1 $\frac{3}{4}$ cups whole wheat
pastry flour

$\frac{1}{4}$ cup cornmeal

$\frac{1}{4}$ cup rye flour

$\frac{1}{4}$ cup brown rice flour

$\frac{1}{4}$ cup barley flour

$\frac{1}{4}$ cup millet flour

2 teaspoons baking
powder

1 teaspoon baking soda

$\frac{1}{4}$ teaspoon sea salt

$\frac{1}{4}$ cup rolled oats

WET INGREDIENTS

1 $\frac{3}{4}$ cups milk

$\frac{1}{2}$ cup canola oil

$\frac{1}{2}$ cup honey

1 tablespoon molasses,
warmed

1 large egg

2 teaspoons grated
lemon peel

GOODIES

1 cup water

$\frac{1}{3}$ cup wheat berries, rinsed

I wanted to create a no-frills multigrain muffin that stands on its own—one that's great with just about everything. Made with seven grains and whole wheat berries, these muffins are the heartiest in the lot. You can also lightly toast the flour for this recipe. After sifting the flours together, place half in a large skillet over a medium flame. Toast for a few minutes or until the flour barely begins to brown. Transfer to a bowl, then toast the remaining flour. Cool to room temperature before using.

1. To prepare the goodie mixture, bring the water to boil in a small saucepan and add the wheat berries. Reduce the heat and simmer 30 minutes, or until the berries are soft and have the texture of cooked brown rice. Remove from the heat, drain any excess liquid, and let cool. (You can prepare the wheat berries earlier and refrigerate until ready to use.)

2. Preheat the oven to 400°F.

3. Sift together all the dry ingredients, except the rolled oats, in a large bowl. Then add the rolled oats and stir to combine.

4. Whisk the wet ingredients in a medium bowl or blend in a food processor. Add the cooked wheat berries to the wet ingredients and stir to combine.

5. Pour the wet mixture into the dry ingredients. Stir just until mixed. *Do not overstir.*

6. Spoon the batter into a greased or papered muffin tin. Fill each cup nearly to the top.

7. Bake for 15 to 20 minutes.

8. Cool the muffins at least 10 minutes before removing from the tin.

Wheat Berry and Date Muffins

Wheat is a fundamental food. The wheat berry is simply whole grain wheat before it has been milled into flour. You could say that all my muffins contain wheat berries because they all contain whole wheat or whole wheat pastry flour. But this muffin spotlights the intact berry. It also calls for dates—another food that has been consumed for centuries.

1. To prepare the goodie mixture, bring the water to boil in a small saucepan and add the wheat berries. Reduce the heat and simmer about 30 minutes, or until the berries are soft and have the texture of cooked brown rice. Remove from the heat, drain any excess liquid, and set aside to cool. Add the dates and stir to combine. (You can prepare the wheat berries earlier and refrigerate until ready to use.)

2. Preheat the oven to 400°F.

3. Sift together all the dry ingredients, except the oats, in a bowl. Then add the oats and stir to combine. Add the goodie mixture and toss to coat.

4. Whisk the wet ingredients in a medium bowl or blend in a food processor. Pour the wet ingredients into the dry mixture. Stir just until mixed. *Do not overstir.*

5. Spoon the batter into a greased or papered muffin tin. Fill each cup nearly to the top.

6. To prepare the topping, mix the brown sugar and cinnamon together in a small bowl. Generously spoon about 1 tablespoon of the topping on each cup of batter, taking care to spread it evenly.

7. Bake for 15 to 20 minutes.

8. Cool the muffins at least 10 minutes before removing from the tin.

YIELD 11–12 MUFFINS

DRY INGREDIENTS

1 cup whole wheat pastry flour
$1/2$ cup whole wheat flour
$1/2$ cup cornmeal
1 teaspoon baking powder
1 teaspoon baking soda
$1/4$ teaspoon sea salt
$1/4$ cup rolled oats

WET INGREDIENTS

1 cup milk
$1/2$ cup applesauce
$1/4$ cup apple butter
1 large egg
1 tablespoon molasses
1 teaspoon grated lemon peel

GOODIES

1 cup water
$1/3$ cup wheat berries, rinsed
$3/4$ cup chopped pitted dates

TOPPING

2 tablespoons dark brown sugar
$1/2$ teaspoon ground cinnamon

7. **Low**-Fat-**and**-Still-Yummy**Muffins**

Jack Sprat could eat no fat;
His wife could eat no lean.

—Mother Goose Nursery Rhyme

O ne Fourth of July not long ago, I met my friend John in Washington, DC. He flew in from Los Angeles to participate in a square dance convention and together we planned to take part in the Independence Day festivities and visit the national monuments. Washington has to be one of the most beautiful cities in the world, and it is especially breathtaking at that time of year.

After taking an early morning subway from the Omni Hotel, where we were staying, to The Ellipse, John and I spent the morning on foot, visiting the White House, Lafayette Park, and various points of interest in that immediate area. Then we decided to walk the several mile touring route around the Tidal Basin and visit each of the monuments. Somewhere between the Washington Monument and the Jefferson Memorial my tootsies began screaming for a rest.

"How 'bout we find a comfy park bench, put our feet up, and feed the pigeons and squirrels for awhile?"

"Sounds good to me."

On our way to an inviting area of the park just on the edge of the basin, we passed an enchanting little refreshment stand—colorful, festive, scalloped umbrella, the whole bit—whose menu included so-called wholesome snacks. I selected a fruit drink and a lemon blueberry muffin. John chose banana nut. As we sat feeling the warmth of friendship and the satisfaction of a delightful morning, I glanced at the nutrition label on the muffin wrapper that I was about to crush and toss into a nearby bin. Fat: 32 grams.

"32 GRAMS!" I exclaimed. "This is a wholesome snack? You've got to be kidding! That's more fat than I want to eat all day!" John's muffin contained the same fat content. He agreed it was indecent. Without a flicker, we put the remains of our muffins back in the wrappers and tossed them in the bin. Bummer. You know what I mean? Bummer.

Baking muffins as I do, I know that that kind of thing just isn't necessary. It's easy to make great-tasting muffins without much fat. Even a light sprinkling of nuts needn't balloon the fat content to 32 grams! If you are watching the fat content in your diet, but don't want to give up muffins, this chapter is especially for you.

Café Crumble Muffins

YIELD
**10–12
MUFFINS**

In a London bakery, I spotted a plain-looking tube-shaped cake with a buttery crumble topping. "What's in that one?" I asked the woman at the counter. "It's coffee cake, Deary," she replied. I asked, "Do you mean it contains coffee or that it is to be enjoyed with coffee?" The woman looked so puzzled at my query (an obvious clash of cultures) that I interrupted her pause with, "Never mind. I'll take a slice." The cake was delightful—and an inspiration for this recipe.

1. Preheat the oven to 400°F.

2. To prepare the crumble topping, combine the flours and brown sugar in a medium bowl. Using a pastry blender or two knives, cut the margarine into the mixture to form crumbles. Set aside.

3. Sift the dry ingredients together in a large bowl.

4. Whisk the wet ingredients in a medium bowl or blend in a food processor. Pour the wet ingredients into the dry ingredients. Stir just until mixed. *Do not overstir.*

5. Spoon the batter into a greased or papered muffin tin. Fill each cup nearly to the top. Top each cup of batter with the crumble topping, taking care to spread it evenly over each cup. Too much topping piled high in the middle will prevent the muffins from rising properly.

6. Bake for 15 to 20 minutes.

7. Cool the muffins at least 10 minutes before removing from the tin.

DRY INGREDIENTS

1 1/2 cups unbleached white flour

1 cup whole wheat flour

1/4 cup light brown sugar

1 1/2 teaspoons baking soda

1 teaspoon baking powder

1/4 teaspoon sea salt

WET INGREDIENTS

1 cup triple-strength coffee, cooled

1/2 cup nonfat yogurt

1/2 cup honey

2 large egg whites

1 1/2 teaspoons vanilla extract

CRUMBLE TOPPING

1/8 cup whole wheat flour

1/4 cup unbleached white flour

3 tablespoons dark brown sugar

2 tablespoons light margarine, softened

Almond-Cardamom-Fig Muffins

YIELD
11–12 MUFFINS

DRY INGREDIENTS

1 1/2 cups whole wheat flour

1 cup unbleached white flour

1/4 cup sugar

1 teaspoon baking powder

1 teaspoon baking soda

1/4 teaspoon sea salt

1/2 teaspoon ground cardamom

WET INGREDIENTS

1 3/4 cups skim milk

3/4 cup applesauce

1 large egg

1 1/2 teaspoons almond extract

1/2 teaspoon vanilla extract

GOODIES

1 cup chopped dried figs

TOPPING

1/2 cup sliced almonds

Dried figs are high in fiber—2.6 grams per ounce, compared to 1.1 grams in raisins and 2.0 grams in prunes. I decided to create a fig muffin, although I wasn't sure I'd be happy with the results. I mean, biting into a particularly seedy dried fig can feel as if you've lost a filling and are crushing it to bits. But the idea of creating a high-fiber muffin was too attractive to pass up. As you will see, with 5.3 grams of fiber, my Almond-Cardamom-Fig Muffins are absolutely delectable.

1. Preheat the oven to 400°F.

2. Sift the dry ingredients together in a large bowl. Add the goodies and toss to coat. If necessary, use your hands to coat the gooey bits.

3. Whisk the wet ingredients in a medium bowl or blend in a food processor. Pour the wet ingredients into the dry mixture. Stir just until mixed. *Do not overstir.*

4. Spoon the batter into a greased or papered muffin tin. Fill each cup nearly to the top. Top each muffin with a large pinch of sliced almonds, taking care to sprinkle them evenly over each cup. Too much topping piled high in the middle will prevent the muffins from rising properly.

5. Bake for 15 to 20 minutes.

6. Cool the muffins at least 10 minutes before removing from the tin.

Apple-Ginger Muffins

YIELD
11–12 MUFFINS

I use crystallized ginger in so many of my muffins that at one point, I worried I might be getting a little carried away. When I find something I really like, I tend to get fanatical and squeeze every ounce of life from it. But after examining my conscience, I decided my fondness for crystallized ginger isn't really a problem. I mean, I'm not obsessed; I just really like it. Like a sip of good cognac, it tingles all the way down to the stomach. And what a fabulous muffin it makes! See for yourself.

1. Preheat the oven to 400°F.

2. Sift the dry ingredients together in a large bowl. Add the goodies and toss to coat.

3. Whisk the wet ingredients in a medium bowl or blend in a food processor. Pour the wet ingredients into the dry mixture. Stir just until mixed. *Do not overstir.*

4. Spoon the batter into a greased or papered muffin tin. Fill each cup nearly to the top.

5. Bake for 15 to 20 minutes.

6. Cool the muffins at least 10 minutes before removing from the tin.

DRY INGREDIENTS

1 cup whole wheat pastry flour

$3/4$ cup whole wheat flour

$3/4$ cup unbleached white flour

1 teaspoon baking powder

1 teaspoon baking soda

$1/4$ teaspoon sea salt

1 teaspoon ground ginger

WET INGREDIENTS

1 $1/2$ cups skim milk

$1/2$ cup applesauce

$1/2$ cup honey

1 large egg

1 teaspoon vanilla extract

1 teaspoon grated lemon peel

GOODIES

1 medium apple, peeled and chopped (do not grate)

3 tablespoons coarsely chopped crystallized ginger

YIELD
12
MUFFINS

DRY INGREDIENTS

$^3/_4$ cup whole wheat
pastry flour

$^3/_4$ cup whole wheat flour

$^3/_4$ cup unbleached
white flour

$^1/_4$ cup light brown sugar

$1 ^1/_2$ teaspoons baking soda

I teaspoon baking powder

$^1/_4$ teaspoon sea salt

$^1/_2$ teaspoon nutmeg

$^1/_4$ cup oat or wheat bran

WET INGREDIENTS

I cup skim milk

$^1/_2$ cup apple juice
concentrate

$^1/_2$ cup nonfat sour cream

$^1/_4$ cup honey

2 large egg whites

I teaspoon vanilla extract

2 teaspoons grated
lemon peel

GOODIES

$^1/_2$ cup dried raspberries

$^1/_2$ cup dried cranberries

Berry Berry Delicious Muffins

When I heard a local store was running a sale on Celestial Seasonings Iced Delight Teas, I hurried right over and bought a few boxes of Caribbean Oasis and Cranberry Razz. After sampling them, I dashed back to buy up the entire stock—twenty-two boxes in all! Now, I'd like to say that I selflessly shared my stash. However, except for an occasional gift, I kept it all for myself. I can't remember when I enjoyed a summer beverage so much. And the Cranberry Razz inspired my Berry Berry Delicious Muffins.

1. Preheat the oven to 400°F.

2. Sift together all the dry ingredients, except the bran, in a large bowl. Then add the bran and stir to combine.

3. Whisk the wet ingredients in a medium bowl or blend in a food processor. Add the goodies and stir to combine.

4. Pour the wet mixture into the dry ingredients. Stir just until mixed. *Do not overstir.*

5. Spoon the batter into a greased or papered muffin tin. Fill each cup nearly to the top.

6. Bake for 15 to 20 minutes.

7. Cool the muffins at least 10 minutes before removing from the tin.

Black Cherry Blossom Muffins

YIELD
10–12 MUFFINS

There's no way around it . . . pitting cherries is a drag, but these muffins are well worth the effort. Start with firm fresh cherries. Cut each in half, remove the pit, then halve each half lengthwise. Finally, cut across the middle of each lengthwise slice to get eight pieces. If cherries are not in season, use pitted canned or frozen varieties. Just be aware that they will bleed into the muffins a bit. Be sure to drain them well before chopping.

1. Preheat the oven to 375°F.

2. Sift together all the dry ingredients, except the bran, in a large bowl. Then add the bran and stir to combine. Add the goodies and toss to coat.

3. Whisk the wet ingredients in a medium bowl or blend in a food processor. Pour the wet ingredients into the dry mixture. Stir just until mixed. *Do not overstir.*

4. Spoon the batter into a greased or papered muffin tin. Fill each cup nearly to the top.

5. Bake for 15 to 20 minutes.

6. Cool the muffins at least 10 minutes before removing from the tin.

DRY INGREDIENTS

1 ½ cups unbleached white flour

1 cup whole wheat flour

2 teaspoons baking soda

½ teaspoon baking powder

¼ teaspoon sea salt

⅛ teaspoon ground mace

¼ cup oat or wheat bran

WET INGREDIENTS

1 ¼ cups skim milk

½ cup applesauce

½ cup honey

2 large egg whites

2 teaspoons grated lemon peel

2 teaspoons cherry flavoring

1 teaspoon vanilla extract

GOODIES

1 cup dark sweet cherries, pitted and chopped

Blueberries, Oats, and Cream Muffins

YIELD
12
MUFFINS

DRY INGREDIENTS

1 ¼ cups whole wheat flour

½ cup unbleached white flour

½ cup light brown sugar

1 teaspoon baking powder

1 ½ teaspoons baking soda

¼ teaspoon sea salt

½ teaspoon ground cinnamon

¾ cup rolled oats

¼ cup oat bran

WET INGREDIENTS

1 ½ cups water

1 cup nonfat sour cream

½ cup honey

1 large egg

2 teaspoons grated lemon peel

1 teaspoon vanilla extract

GOODIES

¾ cup firm fresh blueberries, washed and patted dry

I used to feel guilty about using sour cream, but now that nonfat varieties are available, there's no need for the guilt. Matter of fact, I think nonfat sour cream is nearly as good as the fattier version—at least for baking. And it's wonderful in muffins; it seems to make them lighter without sacrificing richness. I make these muffins with both rolled oats and oat bran to ensure their nutty flavor. Because oats contain a natural antioxidant, these muffins stay fresh longer than those without oats.

1. Preheat the oven to 375°F.

2. Sift together all the dry ingredients, except the rolled oats and oat bran, in a large bowl. Then add the rolled oats and oat bran and stir to combine. Add the goodies and toss to coat.

3. Whisk the wet ingredients in a medium bowl or blend in a food processor. Pour the wet ingredients into the dry mixture. Stir just until mixed. *Do not overstir.*

4. Spoon the batter into a greased or papered muffin tin. Fill each cup nearly to the top.

5. Bake for 15 to 20 minutes.

6. Cool the muffins at least 10 minutes before removing from the tin.

When You Bake, Just Bake

I was watching the chickadees this morning as they visited the Audubon songbird feeder that Donna and Cashin gave me for my birthday. It's a fabulous feeder. The eighteen-or-so-inch clear plastic tube has six portholes and the chickadees perch on small rods extending from each one. Two or three were taking turns poking their heads in the holes and wildly grabbing seed after seed. For every seed they managed to crack between their beaks, a dozen or more were cast about in the frenzy of the feed. (The scene bore a marked similarity to my own groveling about in the sock drawer earlier this morning, casting aside sock after sock as I searched for the mate to the one in my hand.) I watched the birds from my own perch just inside the sliding glass doors of my cottage on the edge of the woods. For the moment, I was relaxed and calm, reflecting upon the sight outside with a certain thoughtfulness.

The birds' frenzy reminded me of those days in the kitchen when I listen to the hurry-up chatter inside my head: "Gotta hurry up. Gotta finish this batch of Chocolate-Almond Muffins, so I can get to the Apple-iscious Apple Spice. Let's see. I've got two hours to bake four dozen muffins and clean up the kitchen. I've gotta work fast, fast, fast."

When I listen to this chatter, I zoom around the kitchen at breakneck speed, so I can finish one thing and get on to the next. Mind you, nothing gets done any faster than it would if I wasn't hurrying. And the simply joy of baking escapes me entirely.

Baking is like meditation. It is most successful when we can muster some semblance of detachment from our inner world; when we are able to notice the chatter of the mind, but not get caught up in it. Then when we bake, we just bake. For the moment, life is as it should be—simple and undisturbed, good enough as it is.

This takes practice. We are in the habit of believing most of the thoughts that pop into our heads, and these thoughts take us in one direction, then another. One moment, we are delirious with delight. Then we are unsatisfied, discontent. Another moment, we are bored with life, uninterested. Contentment always seems to be just out of reach.

When we learn to relate to our inner world as if from our own private cottage on the edge of the woods, we begin to notice that the mind is constantly running. And it doesn't matter which way. The point is, when we stop running with it, we are free to return to the simplicity of what we are doing.

When you bake, just bake. Let all the chatter in your mind disappear into the magic of the moment.

YIELD
12
MUFFINS

Chocolate-Covered Cherry Muffins

DRY INGREDIENTS

1 3/4 cups whole wheat pastry flour

1/2 cup unbleached white flour

1/2 cup cocoa powder

3/4 cup sugar

1 1/2 teaspoons baking powder

1 teaspoon baking soda

1/4 teaspoon sea salt

WET INGREDIENTS

1 1/2 cups skim milk

1/2 cup nonfat sour cream

1/2 cup honey

1 large egg

2 teaspoons cherry flavoring

2 teaspoons vanilla extract

GOODIES

1 cup dark sweet cherries, pitted and chopped

1/2 cup mini semi-sweet chocolate chips

Unlike most chocolate-y treats, these muffins can be made without dairy or refined sugar. Simply replace the skim milk, nonfat sour cream, and chocolate chips with soy milk, soy sour cream, and naturally sweetened chips that contain no dairy. If fresh Bing cherries aren't available, you can use an equivalent amount of frozen dark sweet cherries, although they won't be as plump and firm as fresh ones.

1. Preheat the oven to 400°F.

2. Sift the dry ingredients together in a large bowl. Add the goodies and toss to coat.

3. Whisk the wet ingredients in a medium bowl or blend in a food processor.

4. Pour the wet ingredients into the dry mixture. Stir just until mixed. *Do not overstir.*

5. Spoon the batter into a greased or papered muffin tin. Fill each cup nearly to the top.

6. Bake for 15 to 20 minutes.

7. Cool the muffins at least 10 minutes before removing from the tin.

Chocolate Chip-Banana Muffins

DRY INGREDIENTS

1 1/2 cups unbleached white flour

1 cup whole wheat flour

1/2 cup light brown sugar

1 1/2 teaspoons baking soda

1 teaspoon baking powder

1/4 teaspoon sea salt

WET INGREDIENTS

3 ripe bananas, mashed (1 1/2 cups)

1 cup skim milk

2 large egg whites

2 teaspoons vanilla extract

GOODIES

1/2 cup mini semi-sweet chocolate chips

*If I didn't include a low-fat chocolate chip-banana muffin in **The Complete Muffin Book**, it wouldn't exactly be "complete," would it? As an added treat, try substituting a rich (and expensive!) specialty chocolate for the commercial semi-sweet baking chips in this recipe. Use a food processor or blender to coarsely chop the chocolate. True, this will add a bit more fat, but it will be spread over a dozen or so muffins.*

1. Preheat the oven to 375°F.

2. Sift the dry ingredients together in a large bowl. Add the goodies and toss to coat.

3. Whisk the wet ingredients in a medium bowl or blend in a food processor. Pour the wet ingredients into the dry mixture. Stir just until mixed. *Do not overstir.*

4. Spoon the batter into a greased or papered muffin tin. Fill each cup nearly to the top.

5. Bake for 15 to 20 minutes.

6. Cool the muffins at least 10 minutes before removing from the tin.

YIELD 10–12 MUFFINS

Coco Nana Muffins

DRY INGREDIENTS

1 1/2 cups whole wheat flour

1 cup unbleached white flour

1/2 cup light brown sugar

1 1/2 teaspoons baking powder

1 teaspoon baking soda

1/4 teaspoon sea salt

WET INGREDIENTS

3 ripe bananas, mashed (1 1/2 cups)

1 1/4 cups skim milk

1 large egg

1 tablespoon grated orange peel

1 teaspoon vanilla extract

1 teaspoon coconut extract

GOODIES

3/8 cup flaked coconut

TOPPING

3/8 cup flaked coconut

A low-fat muffin with coconut? Don't be surprised. Coconut isn't the problem you may think it is. This recipe has only 3/4 cup flaked coconut—3/8 cup for the batter and 3/8 cup for the topping. Coconut extract provides extra flavor. Of the 3 grams of fat in each muffin, 2 come from coconut. To me, that's worth it. For muffins with less than 2 fat grams, eliminate the coconut in the batter and use only 3/8 cup as topping. For fat-free muffins, omit the coconut altogether and add 1/2 teaspoon more extract.

1. Preheat the oven to 375°F.

2. Sift the dry ingredients together in a large bowl. Add the goodies and toss to coat.

3. Whisk the wet ingredients in a medium bowl or blend in a food processor. Pour the wet ingredients into the dry mixture. Stir just until mixed. *Do not overstir.*

4. Spoon the batter into a greased or papered muffin tin. Fill each cup nearly to the top. Top each cup of batter with a large pinch of coconut, taking care to sprinkle it evenly over each cup. Too much topping piled high in the middle will prevent the muffins from rising properly.

5. Bake for 15 to 20 minutes.

6. Cool the muffins at least 10 minutes before removing from the tin.

Cottage Cheese and Pear Muffins

YIELD
10–12
MUFFINS

One of Mom's favorite lunches is cottage cheese with sliced pears—a light and delicious low-fat combination that I came to appreciate early in life. Because cottage cheese makes muffins light and airy, and pears are sweet and delicious, I decided to translate this meal into a delectable muffin. And it doesn't matter if you use fresh pears or canned. Both hold their texture and flavor equally well.

1. Preheat the oven to 400°F.

2. Sift the dry ingredients together in a large bowl.

3. Whisk the wet ingredients in a medium bowl. Do not use a food processor to combine the wet ingredients. Add the goodies and stir to combine.

4. Pour the wet mixture into the dry ingredients. Stir just until mixed. *Do not overstir.*

5. Spoon the batter into a greased or papered muffin tin. Fill each cup nearly to the top.

6. Bake for 15 to 20 minutes

7. Cool the muffins at least 10 minutes before removing from the tin.

DRY INGREDIENTS

1 cup whole wheat flour

1 cup unbleached white flour

1/4 cup light brown sugar

1 teaspoon baking powder

1 teaspoon baking soda

1/4 teaspoon sea salt

1/2 teaspoon ground cardamom

WET INGREDIENTS

1 cup nonfat cottage cheese

1/2 cup skim milk

1/2 cup apple juice concentrate

1 tablespoon canola oil

2 large egg whites

1/2 cup honey

GOODIES

2 small pears, peeled and chopped

Cranberry-Apple Muffins

**YIELD
12
MUFFINS**

DRY INGREDIENTS

1 cup whole wheat pastry flour

$3/4$ cup whole wheat flour

$3/4$ cup unbleached white flour

$1/4$ cup light brown sugar

1 teaspoon baking powder

1 teaspoon baking soda

$1/4$ teaspoon sea salt

1 teaspoon ground cinnamon

WET INGREDIENTS

1 $1/4$ cups nonfat buttermilk

$1/2$ cup apple juice concentrate

$1/2$ cup honey

2 large egg whites

2 teaspoons grated orange peel

1 teaspoon rum extract

GOODIES

1 cup chopped fresh apples

$3/4$ cup dried cranberries

One Christmas, I made cranberry-apple conserve from a recipe I found on the Internet. It was a great new condiment for our holiday dinner—a delicious alternative to my usual cranberry-orange relish or Mom's cranberry sauce. I liked it so much, I had it every morning for a week with yogurt and a pumpkin muffin. Of course, my "muffin mind" saw the possibilities, and I set about the task of creating this basic all-around muffin. Light Brown Sugar Glaze (page 192) makes a great topping.

1. Preheat the oven to 400°F.

2. Sift the dry ingredients together in a large bowl.

3. Whisk the wet ingredients in a medium bowl or blend in a food processor. Add the goodies and toss to coat.

4. Pour the wet mixture into the dry ingredients. Stir just until mixed. *Do not overstir.*

5. Spoon the batter into a greased or papered muffin tin. Fill each cup nearly to the top.

6. Bake for 15 to 20 minutes.

7. Cool the muffins at least 10 minutes before removing from the tin.

Double Ginger Ginger Muffins

YIELD
10–12
MUFFINS

Here's another installment in my crystallized ginger series. Clocking in at less than 1 gram of fat per muffin, and deriving only 3 percent of their calories from fat, these Double Ginger Ginger Muffins are excellent for those times when you want a low-fat breakfast or snack.

1. Preheat the oven to 400°F.

2. Sift the dry ingredients together in a large bowl.

3. Whisk the wet ingredients in a medium bowl or blend in a food processor. Add the goodies and stir to combine.

4. Pour the wet mixture into the dry ingredients. Stir just until mixed. *Do not overstir.*

5. Spoon the batter into a greased or papered muffin tin. Fill each cup nearly to the top.

6. Bake for 15 to 20 minutes.

7. Cool the muffins at least 10 minutes before removing from the tin.

DRY INGREDIENTS

1 cup whole wheat flour

1 cup unbleached white flour

$1/2$ cup brown rice flour

$1 1/2$ teaspoons baking soda

1 teaspoon baking powder

1 tablespoon ground ginger

$3/4$ teaspoon ground cinnamon

$1/2$ teaspoon ground nutmeg

$1/4$ teaspoon sea salt

WET INGREDIENTS

1 cup skim milk

$1/2$ cup water

$1/4$ cup honey

$1/4$ cup molasses

2 large egg whites

1 tablespoon grated orange peel

GOODIES

3 tablespoons coarsely chopped crystallized ginger

$1/2$ cup golden raisins

YIELD
12
MUFFINS

DRY INGREDIENTS

1 cup whole wheat pastry flour

1 cup unbleached white flour

1/2 cup whole wheat flour

1/4 cup dark brown sugar

1 1/2 teaspoons baking soda

1 teaspoon baking powder

1/4 teaspoon sea salt

1 teaspoon ground cinnamon

1/2 teaspoon ground cloves

1/4 teaspoon ground nutmeg

1/2 cup oat or wheat bran

WET INGREDIENTS

1 1/4 cups skim milk

1 cup sweet potato purée*

2 large egg whites

1/4 cup molasses

2 teaspoons grated orange peel

Hillsborough House Inn Breakfast Muffins

I created this muffin for Katherine and Bev Webb, owners of North Carolina's historic Hillsborough House Inn. While staying at this magnificent inn (circa 1790) with its enormous wraparound porch, candlelit parlors, and bedrooms filled with historic memorabilia, I felt the presence of the many residents and visitors who had been there before me. And I was so impressed by the warmth and hospitality of its owners that I had to create a muffin for them. This recipe has a little bit of North Carolina (sweet potatoes), a little bit of old country magic (currants), and lots of the sweet joy of friendship. For directions on preparing the sweet potato purée, see the recipe for Caribbean Sweet Potato Gingerbread Muffins on page 122.

1. To prepare the topping, combine the nuts, wheat germ, and brown sugar in a small bowl. Add the softened margarine and stir to combine. Set aside.

2. Preheat the oven to 400°F.

3. Sift together all the dry ingredients, except the bran, in a large bowl. Then add the bran and stir to combine.

4. Whisk the wet ingredients in a medium bowl or blend in a food processor. Add the goodies and stir to combine.

5. Pour the wet ingredients into the dry ingredients. Stir just until mixed. *Do not overstir.*

6. Spoon the batter into a greased or papered muffin tin. Fill each cup nearly to the top. Top each cup of batter with the topping mixture, taking care to spread it evenly over each cup. Too much topping piled high in the middle will prevent the muffins from rising properly.

7. Bake for 15 to 20 minutes.

8. Cool the muffins at least 10 minutes before removing from the tin.

GOODIES

½ cup currants

TOPPING

¼ cup coarsely chopped roasted walnuts

½ cup honey crunch wheat germ

¼ cup dark brown sugar

1 tablespoon margarine, softened

Orange-Strawberry-Banana Muffins

DRY INGREDIENTS

1 $\frac{1}{2}$ cups whole wheat flour

1 cup unbleached white flour

$\frac{1}{2}$ cup light brown sugar

1 teaspoon baking powder

1 teaspoon baking soda

$\frac{1}{2}$ teaspoon ground nutmeg

$\frac{1}{4}$ teaspoon sea salt

$\frac{1}{2}$ cup oat bran

WET INGREDIENTS

2 ripe bananas, mashed (1 cup)

1 cup skim milk

2 large egg whites

1 tablespoon grated orange peel

3 teaspoons strawberry flavoring

1 teaspoon vanilla extract

Fresh strawberries don't hold up in muffins. If you cut them into bite-sized pieces, they turn to mush as the muffins bake and the batter around them becomes spongy and gooey. If you purée them, the muffins will turn a funny purplish brown color—very unappetizing. And, most important, the strawberry flavor just doesn't come through. Anyway, these muffins are made with strawberry flavoring instead of fresh strawberries. Take my word for it . . . or learn it for yourself.

1. Preheat the oven to 375°F.

2. Sift together all the dry ingredients, except the bran, in a large bowl. Then add the bran and stir to combine.

3. Whisk the wet ingredients in a medium bowl or blend in a food processor. Pour the wet ingredients into the dry mixture. Stir just until mixed. *Do not overstir.*

4. Spoon the batter into a greased or papered muffin tin. Fill each cup nearly to the top.

5. Bake for 15 to 20 minutes.

6. Cool the muffins at least 10 minutes before removing from the tin.

Pineapple-Carrot-Ginger Muffins

For me, hot fudge sundaes, baked Brie with almonds, and carrot cake are among life's essentials. Surely one can't expect to survive without carrot cake! But with an expanding middle-age waistline, how do I justify eating traditional carrot cake with butter and cream cheese icing? The answer is: I don't, I can't. I won't (at least not often). To satisfy this "need," I created these muffins, which contain only 2 grams of fat each. I enjoy them plain or with Vanilla Cream Cheese Icing (page 193).

1. Preheat the oven to 400°F.

2. Sift the dry ingredients together in a large bowl. Add the goodies and toss to coat.

3. Whisk the wet ingredients in a medium bowl or blend in a food processor. Pour the wet ingredients into the dry mixture. Stir just until mixed. *Do not overstir.*

4. Spoon the batter into a greased or papered muffin tin. Fill each cup nearly to the top.

5. Bake for 15 to 20 minutes.

6. Cool the muffins at least 10 minutes before removing from the tin.

YIELD
11–12 MUFFINS

DRY INGREDIENTS
1 1/4 cups whole wheat flour

1 1/4 cups unbleached white flour

1/2 cup light brown sugar

1 1/2 teaspoons baking soda

1 teaspoon baking powder

1 teaspoon powdered ginger

1/4 teaspoon sea salt

WET INGREDIENTS
1 1/2 cups skim milk

1/4 cup apple juice concentrate

1 tablespoon canola oil

1 large egg

1 teaspoon grated orange peel

GOODIES
1/2 cup grated carrots

1/2 cup chopped dried pineapple

2 tablespoons grated ginger root

Ricotta Cheese with Basil and Rosemary Muffins

YIELD
11–12 MUFFINS

DRY INGREDIENTS

I cup whole wheat flour

I cup unbleached white flour

$\frac{1}{2}$ cup rye flour

I $\frac{1}{2}$ teaspoons baking powder

I teaspoon baking soda

$\frac{1}{4}$ teaspoon sea salt

WET INGREDIENTS

I cup low-fat ricotta cheese

I cup vegetable broth

$\frac{1}{2}$ cup skim milk

I tablespoon olive oil

I large egg

GOODIES

4 teaspoons chopped fresh basil, or 2 teaspoons dried

I teaspoon chopped fresh rosemary, or $\frac{1}{2}$ teaspoon dried

My brother-in-law Bob is often found holding the refrigerator door open with his right hip, a carton of ricotta cheese in one hand, a tablespoon in the other, and cheeks bulging as he savors this late-night snack. My niece Laura says she can hear him mmm-ing with delight two rooms away. That's how it is with ricotta lovers. There's only one thing that can heighten the pleasure further—a touch of fresh basil and rosemary. Even if you're not a fan of ricotta, you'll find these muffins hard to resist.

1. Preheat the oven to 400°F.

2. Sift all the dry ingredients together in a large bowl. Add the goodies and toss to coat.

3. Whisk the wet ingredients in a medium bowl. Do not use a food processor to combine the wet ingredients. Pour the wet ingredients into the dry mixture. Stir just until mixed. *Do not overstir.*

4. Spoon the batter into a greased or papered muffin tin. Fill each cup nearly to the top.

5. Bake for 15 to 20 minutes

6. Cool the muffins at least 10 minutes before removing from the tin.

Scarborough Fair Muffins

One Christmas, I received three pottery jars that held sage, rosemary, and thyme plants. I placed them on the shelf above the stove. One day, I was in the kitchen baking when I realized I was singing "Scarborough Fair." I glanced at the shelf and knew what had triggered the song. Paul Simon came to mind. I wanted to write and thank him for being the poet laureate of my life, but I never did. I thanked him with my Scarborough Fair Muffins instead. He writes songs, I create muffins.

1. Preheat the oven to 400°F.

2. Sift the dry ingredients together in a large bowl. Add the goodies and toss to coat.

3. Whisk the wet ingredients in a medium bowl or blend in a food processor. Pour the wet ingredients into the dry mixture. Stir just until mixed. *Do not overstir.*

4. Spoon the batter into a greased or papered muffin tin. Fill each cup nearly to the top.

5. Bake for 15 to 20 minutes.

6. Cool the muffins at least 10 minutes before removing from the tin.

DRY INGREDIENTS

1 1/2 cups whole wheat pastry flour

1/2 cup whole wheat flour

1/2 cup unbleached white flour

1/2 cup rye flour

2 teaspoons baking powder

1 teaspoon baking soda

1/4 teaspoon sea salt

WET INGREDIENTS

1 cup vegetable broth

1/2 cup nonfat buttermilk

1/4 cup water

2 tablespoons honey

1 tablespoon olive oil

1 large egg

1 teaspoon grated lemon peel

GOODIES

1 1/2 teaspoons chopped fresh sage, or 3/4 teaspoon dried

1 1/2 teaspoons chopped fresh rosemary, or 3/4 teaspoon dried

1 1/2 teaspoons chopped fresh thyme, or 3/4 teaspoon dried

Toasted Wheat Germ Crunch Muffins

YIELD
11–12
MUFFINS

DRY INGREDIENTS

1 $\frac{1}{4}$ cups whole wheat flour

1 $\frac{1}{4}$ cups unbleached white flour

1 tablespoon soy flour

1 $\frac{1}{2}$ teaspoons baking soda

1 teaspoon baking powder

$\frac{1}{4}$ teaspoon sea salt

WET INGREDIENTS

1 cup nonfat buttermilk

$\frac{1}{2}$ cup water

$\frac{1}{4}$ cup apple juice concentrate

$\frac{1}{4}$ cup maple syrup

2 large egg whites

1 teaspoon vanilla extract

TOPPING

1 cup honey crunch wheat germ

$\frac{1}{2}$ cup light brown sugar

2 tablespoons light margarine, softened

Whole grain wheat—the seed of the wheat plant—is made up of the germ, endosperm, and bran. These muffins spotlight the nutty flavor and wholesome goodness of the germ. Rich in vitamins and minerals (especially vitamin E, calcium, and magnesium), wheat germ has a high oil content, making it vulnerable to spoilage. To protect the germ and delay spoilage, it is often toasted and stored in airtight containers. You can find toasted wheat germ in the cereal aisle of your grocery store.

1. Preheat the oven to 400°F.

2. Sift the dry ingredients together in a large bowl.

3. To prepare the topping, combine the nuts, wheat germ, and brown sugar in a medium bowl and stir to combine. Add the margarine and stir well. Retain $\frac{3}{4}$ cup of the mixture to top each muffin (see Step 5). Add the remaining mixture to the dry ingredients and stir to combine.

4. Whisk the wet ingredients in a medium bowl or blend in a food processor. Pour the wet ingredients into the dry mixture. Stir just until mixed. *Do not overstir.*

5. Spoon the batter into a greased or papered muffin tin. Fill each cup nearly to the top. Top each cup of batter with the reserved topping, taking care to spread it evenly over each cup. Too much topping piled high in the middle will prevent the muffins from rising properly.

6. Bake for 15 to 20 minutes.

7. Cool the muffins at least 10 minutes before removing from the tin.

8. **Top**-Notch **Toppings**

Having well polished the whole bow,
he added a golden tip.

—HOMER, *ILIAD*, BOOK IV

Every muffin in this book can stand on its own two feet. That is, they are delicious without any additions—not even butter! But that doesn't mean we can't add a little something extra. Right? That's why I created this tasty selection of butters, spreads, glazes, and icings.

I have placed these recipes (each of which yields enough for about a dozen muffins) in a separate chapter because I didn't want to confine their use to any one muffin. I hope you'll try every one of the toppings in this chapter, mixing and matching them with your favorite home-baked muffins.

Throughout the book, however, I have offered suggested toppings for many of the muffin recipes. These recommendations are the result of many years of personal experience, and I couldn't help but share them with you. For instance, I believe Maple Butter Spread is absolutely awesome on Breakfast Boston Brown Muffins, while Eat-Your-Oatmeal Muffins topped with Honey Cinnamon Spread or Apple Butter Spread is simply unbeatable. Although the Very Berry Bran Muffins and my Old Fashioned Ginger-Currant Muffins are delicious plain, when topped with Lemony Lemon Spread, they reach flavorful new heights. To magnify the already delicious nutty, chocolaty flavor of Roger's Chocolate Fruit-and-Nut Muffins, I suggest crowning them with some Chocolate-Peanut Butter Spread—it'll knock your socks off. And the Orange Glaze adds a mouthwatering dimension to my Glazed Orange-Carrot Muffins. But don't use these toppings exclusively on the muffins that I've recommended. Try them on any muffins you'd like, as well as on your toast or croissants (when no one is looking!).

Be aware that there are some basic rules to follow when applying icings, glazes, and spreads. Always be sure the muffins are completely cool before adding icing. If not, the icing will do a disappearing act and melt its way right into the muffin. This isn't an awful outcome; it's just not what you had in mind. The muffins *can*, however, be warm before adding glazes or spreads; just be sure you've let them cool the usual ten minutes after removing them from the oven.

So unleash your creativity! Feel free to try out my "muffin-and-topping" suggestions or follow your instincts and come up with your own luscious combinations. There is no right or wrong here. So go for it!

Apple Butter Spread

YIELD
ABOUT $3/4$ CUP

INGREDIENTS

4 ounces cream cheese, softened

$1/4$ cup apple butter

1 teaspoon grated fresh ginger root, or $1/2$ teaspoon ground

1. Cream the ingredients together in a small bowl.

2. Use immediately, or refrigerate until ready to use.

Chocolate-Peanut Butter Spread

YIELD
ABOUT $3/4$ CUP

INGREDIENTS

$1/2$ cup smooth peanut butter

2 tablespoons cocoa

1 tablespoon canola oil

$1/4$ cup honey

1. Blend the ingredients together in a small bowl.

2. Use immediately, or refrigerate until ready to use.

Peanut Butter and Apple Butter Spread

YIELD
ABOUT $3/4$ CUP

INGREDIENTS

$1/4$ cup smooth peanut butter

$1/2$ cup apple butter

1. Blend the ingredients together in a small bowl.

2. Spread onto cooled muffins.

YIELD
ABOUT ½ CUP

INGREDIENTS

½ cup margarine or butter, softened

1 tablespoon honey

½ teaspoon ground cinnamon

Honey Cinnamon Spread

1. Cream the ingredients together in a small bowl.

2. Use immediately, or refrigerate until ready to use.

YIELD
ABOUT ½ CUP

INGREDIENTS

½ cup margarine, butter, or cream cheese, softened

3 tablespoons lemon juice

2 tablespoons warm honey

1 teaspoon finely grated lemon peel

Lemony Lemon Spread

1. Cream the ingredients together in a small bowl.

2. Use immediately, or refrigerate until ready to use.

YIELD
ABOUT ½ CUP

INGREDIENTS

½ cup margarine or butter, softened

6 tablespoons pure maple syrup

Maple Butter Spread

1. Cream the ingredients together in a small bowl.

2. Use immediately, or refrigerate until ready to use.

Sweet and Fruity Spread

YIELD
ABOUT 1 CUP

INGREDIENTS

$\frac{1}{2}$ cup margarine or butter, softened

$\frac{1}{2}$ cup all-fruit jam, jelly, or marmalade

$\frac{1}{2}$ teaspoon finely grated lemon peel

1. Cream the ingredients together in a small bowl.

2. Use immediately, or refrigerate until ready to use.

Orange Glaze

YIELD
ABOUT $\frac{1}{2}$ CUP

INGREDIENTS

I tablespoon cornstarch

$\frac{1}{4}$ cup orange juice

3 tablespoons margarine or butter

3 tablespoons honey

1. Place the orange juice in a small bowl, add the cornstarch, and stir to dissolve.

2. Melt the margarine in a small saucepan over medium heat, then add the cornstarch mixture.

3. Bring to a boil, then reduce the heat to low. Stirring constantly, cook until the glaze thickens and becomes clear. Remove from the heat.

4. Allow the glaze to cool a minute or two before spreading it warm on the cooled muffins.

Citrus Honey Glaze

YIELD
ABOUT ½ CUP

INGREDIENTS

1 tablespoon cornstarch

½ cup lemonade or orange juice

¼ cup honey

½ teaspoon finely grated lemon or orange peel

1. Place the cornstarch and lemonade in a small saucepan and stir to dissolve. Add the honey and citrus peel.

2. Bring the mixture to a boil, then reduce the heat to low. Stirring constantly, cook until the glaze thickens and becomes clear. Remove from the heat.

3. Allow the glaze to cool a minute or two before spreading it warm on the cooled muffins.

Light Brown Sugar Glaze

YIELD
ABOUT ½ CUP

INGREDIENTS

5 tablespoons margarine or butter

3 tablespoons light brown sugar

1. Melt the margarine in a small saucepan over low heat. Add the brown sugar.

2. Stirring constantly, heat the mixture until the brown sugar melts and the glaze is smooth. Remove from the heat.

3. Allow the glaze to cool a minute or two before spreading it warm on the cooled muffins.

Maple Cream Cheese Icing

YIELD
ABOUT $^3/_4$ CUP

INGREDIENTS

4 ounces cream cheese, softened

1 cup confectioners sugar

2 tablespoons maple syrup

1. Cream the ingredients together in a small bowl.

2. Spread onto cooled muffins.

Coffee Icing

YIELD
ABOUT $^3/_4$ CUP

INGREDIENTS

$^1/_2$ cup margarine or butter, softened

1 cup confectioners sugar

2 tablespoons strong coffee

1 teaspoon vanilla extract

1. Cream the ingredients together in a small bowl.

2. Spread onto cooled muffins.

Vanilla Cream Cheese Icing

YIELD
ABOUT $^3/_4$ CUP

INGREDIENTS

4 ounces cream cheese, softened

1 tablespoon margarine or butter, softened

1 teaspoon vanilla extract

1. Cream the ingredients together in a small bowl.

2. Spread onto cooled muffins.

Metric Conversion Tables

Common Liquid Conversions

Measurement	=	Milliliters
$1/4$ teaspoon	=	1.25 milliliters
$1/2$ teaspoon	=	2.50 milliliters
$3/4$ teaspoon	=	3.75 milliliters
1 teaspoon	=	5.00 milliliters
$1 1/4$ teaspoons	=	6.25 milliliters
$1 1/2$ teaspoons	=	7.50 milliliters
$1 3/4$ teaspoons	=	8.75 milliliters
2 teaspoons	=	10.0 milliliters
1 tablespoon	=	15.0 milliliters
2 tablespoons	=	30.0 milliliters

Measurement	=	Liters
$1/4$ cup	=	0.06 liters
$1/2$ cup	=	0.12 liters
$3/4$ cup	=	0.18 liters
1 cup	=	0.24 liters
$1 1/4$ cups	=	0.30 liters
$1 1/2$ cups	=	0.36 liters
2 cups	=	0.48 liters
$2 1/2$ cups	=	0.60 liters
3 cups	=	0.72 liters
$3 1/2$ cups	=	0.84 liters
4 cups	=	0.96 liters
$4 1/2$ cups	=	1.08 liters
5 cups	=	1.20 liters
$5 1/2$ cups	=	1.32 liters

Conversion Formulas

LIQUID

When You Know	Multiply By	To Determine
teaspoons	5.0	milliliters
tablespoons	15.0	milliliters
fluid ounces	30.0	milliliters
cups	0.24	liters
pints	0.47	liters
quarts	0.95	liters

WEIGHT

When You Know	Multiply By	To Determine
ounces	28.0	grams
pounds	0.45	kilograms

Converting Fahrenheit to Celsius

Fahrenheit	=	Celsius
200–205	=	95
220–225	=	105
245–250	=	120
275	=	135
300–305	=	150
325–330	=	165
345–350	=	175
370–375	=	190
400–405	=	205
425–430	=	220
445–450	=	230
470–475	=	245
500	=	260

Quick Recipe Reference

The following guide alphabetically lists (in chapter order) all of the muffin recipes found in *The Complete Muffin Cookbook* along with their defining ingredients. This guide will help you easily select a recipe that contains a specific ingredient (or ingredients) you desire.

2. Get-Up-and-Go Muffins

The following muffins were made with breakfast in mind, but they are great any time.

Apple-Orange-Oat Bran Muffins. Fresh apples, applesauce, oat bran, and a touch of orange peel and spices.

Better Banana Nut Bran Muffins. Ripe bananas, wheat bran, and roasted walnuts.

Blueberry Blintz Muffins. Fresh blueberries, ricotta cheese, sour cream, oat flour, and a touch of lemon peel.

Blue Morning Muffins. Fresh blueberries, yellow or blue cornmeal, coconut, applesauce, and all-fruit blueberry jam.

Breakfast Boston Brown Muffins. Yellow cornmeal, buckwheat flour, roasted sunflower seeds, raisins, and apple juice concentrate.

Buckwheat Buttermilk Muffins with Blueberries and Maple Syrup. Buckwheat flour, buttermilk, fresh blueberries, maple syrup, and a hint of orange peel.

California Mix Muffins. Dried fruit, ripe bananas, and a hint of lemon peel.

Catherine's Lemon-Red Raspberry Muffins. Fresh raspberries, applesauce, buttermilk, and lemon peel.

Cherry Irish Soda Muffins. Dried cherries, currants, orange and lemon peel, caraway seeds, and buttermilk.

Crazy Raisin Muffins. Lots of raisins with honey, orange peel, and spices.

Crunchy Granola Crumble Muffins. Granola, applesauce, buttermilk, maple syrup, and a hint of orange peel and spice.

Eat-Your-Oatmeal Muffins. Rolled oats, fresh apples or pears, roasted sunflower seeds, raisins, and spices.

Fakin' Bacon Muffins. Fakin' bacon, buttermilk, and onion.

Friends-of-the-Earth Vegan Muffins. Dates, dried fruit bits, roasted walnuts, ripe bananas, soy milk, and a hint of lemon peel and spices.

Ladda's Lemon Ginger Muffins. Fresh ginger root, lemon peel, and spice.

Maple Pecan Muffins. Roasted pecans, maple syrup, barley flour, buttermilk, and malted milk powder.

Only-Kids-Need-Apply Muffins. Chunky peanut butter, semi-sweet chocolate or carob chips, and toasted wheat germ.

Peanut Butter-Rice Cake Muffins. Chunky peanut butter, ripe bananas, raisins, roasted sunflower seeds, and spice.

Proof-of-the-Pudding Muffins. Yellow cornmeal, fresh ginger root, raisins, orange peel, molasses, and spices.

Raspberry Bouquet Muffins. Fresh raspberries, apple juice concentrate, all-fruit raspberry jam, and lemon peel.

Soysage Cheese Muffins. Soysage, buttermilk, cheddar cheese, and herbs.

Start-a-Movement Muffins. Prunes, wheat bran, apple juice concentrate, molasses, and a hint of orange peel.

Thanks-to-the-Tropical-Sun Muffins. Fresh mango, dried papaya, apricot all-fruit jam, and a hint of lemon peel.

Very Berry Bran Muffins. Fresh berries, wheat bran, buttermilk, spices, and a hint of lemon peel.

3. Crunchy, Crumbly, Spicy Do-Da Muffins

These muffins are great with fresh-brewed coffee or tea.

Almond Delight Muffins. Roasted almonds, sour cream, dark brown sugar, and spices.

Apple-Walnut Crumble Muffins. Fresh apples, applesauce, buttermilk, roasted walnuts, spices, and a crumble topping.

Apple-iscious Apple Spice Muffins. Fresh apples, applesauce, apple butter, lemon peel, spice, and a honey crunch wheat germ topping.

Apricot-Sesame Muffins. Apricot purée, dried apricots, buttermilk, and a sprinkling of sesame seeds.

Carrot Conglomeration Muffins. Fresh apples, carrots, raisins, roasted sunflower seeds, coconut, apple juice concentrate, orange peel, and spice—everything but the kitchen sink.

Chai Muffins. Chai tea and honey, Honey!

Citrus Yogurt-Poppy Seed Muffins. Plain yogurt, lemon or orange peel, and poppy seeds.

Cracked-Up Wheat Muffins. Bulgur, dried apples, apple juice concentrate, and spice.

Dad's Summer Squash Muffins. Yellow squash or zucchini, roasted walnuts, raisins, spice, and a hint of molasses.

Far East Muffins. Vanilla yogurt, lemon peel, and lots of spices.

Lemon Pecan Muffins. Roasted pecans, lemon peel, apple juice concentrate, and buttermilk.

Mango with Crystallized Ginger Muffins. Mango purée, crystallized ginger, lemon peel, and a hint of rum flavoring.

Mom's Applesauce Muffins. Chunky applesauce, dates, raisins, roasted walnuts, and spices.

Orange Cardamom Muffins. Buttermilk, honey, orange peel, and cardamom.

Peachy Peach Muffins. Peach purée, dried peaches, all-fruit peach jam, and a hint of orange peel.

Prune Spice Muffins. Prunes, roasted walnuts, buttermilk, apple juice concentrate, cinnamon, allspice, and cloves.

Seven-Factors-of-Enlightenment Muffins. Applesauce, brown sugar, granola, chocolate or carob chips, flaked coconut, roasted walnuts, and sunflower seeds.

Spice Muffins with Vanilla Cream Cheese Icing. Applesauce, golden raisins, buttermilk, orange peel, and lots of spice.

Triple-Apricot Ambrosia Muffins. Apricot purée and dried apricots with a topping of all-fruit apricot preserves and flaked coconut.

Tropical Fruit Muffins. Dried tropical fruit mix (pineapple, apricots, coconut, papaya, raisins, golden raisins, apples), with fresh bananas, orange peel, and a hint of rum flavoring.

4. Herby Cheesy Muffin Thangs

The following muffins, made with cheeses, flavorful herbs, and a variety of other interesting thangs, are perfect meal accompaniments.

Artichoke Hearts with Basil Muffins. Artichoke hearts, vegetable broth, Parmesan cheese, garlic, and fresh basil.

Barley-Mushroom Muffins. Whole grain barley, barley flour, mushrooms, onion, carrots, vegetable broth, and nutritional yeast flakes.

Béarnaise Muffins. Tarragon, Dijon mustard, chopped chives, soy sauce, and vegetable broth.

Brie-with-Brandy Muffins. Brie, slivered almonds, golden raisins, brown sugar, and brandy flavoring.

Cashew Curry Muffins. Roasted cashews, fresh apples, raisins, coconut, garlic, fresh ginger root, curry powder, and vegetable broth.

Chutney Muffins. Your favorite chutney!

Cosmic Cottage Dill Muffins. Cottage cheese, dill seeds, and onion.

French Onion Muffins. Onion, vegetable broth, nutritional yeast flakes, garlic, Swiss cheese, soy sauce, Dijon mustard, and tarragon.

Garden Vegetable Cream Cheese Muffins. Cream cheese with garden vegetables, mixed herbs, and sautéed onion.

Hushpuppy Muffins. Cornmeal (yellow, white, or blue), sour cream, sautéed onion, and white or yellow corn.

Jewish Rye Muffins. Rye flour, rye flakes, and caraway seeds.

Mama Mia Muffins. Parmesan cheese, garlic, vegetable broth, basil, and oregano.

Mexicali Corn Muffins. Yellow cornmeal, buttermilk, jalapeño peppers, pimento, and corn.

Nickerpumpel Muffins. Buckwheat flour, dark rye flour, molasses, and caraway seeds.

Pesto Muffins. Fresh basil, garlic, roasted walnuts, Parmesan cheese, vegetable broth, olive oil, and buttermilk.

Roasted Red Pepper Muffins. Brown rice flour, garlic-herb cream cheese, roasted red peppers, and rosemary.

Seedy Muffins. Seeds galore—caraway, sesame, roasted sunflower, poppy—garlic, and tahini.

Soysage Pizza Muffins. Soysage, sun-dried tomatoes, mozzarella cheese, garlic, tomato juice, olive oil, and Italian herbs.

Spanakopita Muffins. Cottage cheese, feta cheese, chopped spinach, garlic, vegetable broth, and ground mace.

Spring Roll Muffins. Celery, scallion, water chestnuts, ginger root, dried apricots, soy sauce, and toasted sesame oil.

Steven's Sun-Dried Tomato Muffins. Sun-dried tomatoes, pine nuts, Parmesan cheese, chopped spinach, tomato juice, and Italian herbs.

Stuffin' Muffins. Celery, onions, roasted walnuts, roasted sunflower seeds, raisins, sharp cheddar cheese, and vegetable broth.

Sun-Dried Tomato Corn Muffins with Cumin. Yellow or white cornmeal, sun-dried tomatoes, tomato juice, buttermilk, and cumin seeds.

Tomato Basil Muffins. Sun-dried tomatoes, tomato juice, garlic, and fresh basil.

Waldorf Muffins. Fresh apples, dried apples, celery, roasted walnuts, raisins, apple juice concentrate, and a hint of lemon peel.

5. Holiday and Special Occasion Muffins

Interesting dessert-y ingredients make these muffins great for special occasions—or no occasion at all!

Amaretto Muffins. Barley flour, dark sweet cherries, buttermilk, and Amaretto flavoring, with pearl sugar and sliced almond topping.

Anise Orange Muffins. Cottage cheese, honey, anise seeds, and orange peel.

Banana Nut Fudge Muffins. Ripe bananas, fresh brewed coffee, and mini semi-sweet chocolate chips, with roasted walnuts and egg white topping.

Bananas Foster Muffins. Ripe bananas, brandy flavoring, and sour cream, with a honey crunch wheat germ topping.

Blackberry Cheesecake Muffins. Fresh blackberries, cream cheese, sour cream, and lemon peel.

Butterscotch Pecan Muffins. Roasted pecans, butterscotch chips, butterscotch syrup, dark brown sugar, and sour cream.

Caribbean Sweet Potato Gingerbread Muffins. Sweet potato purée, fresh ginger root, molasses, orange peel, and spices.

Chocolate-Almond Muffins. Mini semi-sweet chocolate chips, cocoa powder, sour cream, and sliced almonds.

Chocolate-Ginger Muffins. Brown rice flour, cocoa powder, crystallized ginger, and buttermilk.

Chocolate Raspberry Chambord Muffins. Fresh raspberries, mini semi-sweet chocolate chips, cocoa powder, buttermilk, and raspberry liqueur.

Classic Colada Muffins. Flaked coconut, crushed pineapple, and apple juice concentrate.

Cranberry-Orange Muffins. Cranberries, roasted walnuts, orange marmalade, and orange peel.

Double Chocolate Chocolate Muffins. Cocoa powder, mini semi-sweet chocolate chips, milk chocolate, and buttermilk.

Down-to-Earth Date-and-Nut Muffins. Dates, flaked coconut, roasted almonds, buttermilk, molasses, and orange peel.

Easy-Living Southern Pecan Muffins. Roasted pecans, light brown sugar, and margarine or butter.

Fruitcake Muffins. Mixed dried fruit, mixed roasted nuts and seeds, ripe bananas, molasses, and orange peel.

Lyman's Chocolate Cheesecake Muffins. Mini semi-sweet chocolate chips, cocoa powder, cream cheese, and sour cream.

Mocha Chip Muffins. Triple-strength coffee, mini semi-sweet chocolate chips, roasted walnuts, and butter.

Mincemeat Muffins. Mincemeat and buttermilk.

Old Fashioned Ginger-Currant Muffins. Fresh ginger root, currants, buttermilk, apple juice concentrate, molasses, and spices.

Orange-Chocolate Muffins. Mini semi-sweet chocolate chips and orange peel.

Patty's Reincarnated Cappuccino Muffins. Triple-strength coffee, cocoa powder, sour cream, cinnamon.

Pistachio and Dried Cranberry Muffins. Dried cranberries, roasted pistachios, apple juice concentrate, and sour cream.

Pumpkin-Chocolate Chip Muffins. Pumpkin purée, mini semi-sweet chocolate chips, roasted walnuts, and lots of spices.

Pumpkin-Pumpkin Seed Muffins. Pumpkin purée, roasted pumpkin seeds, raisins, molasses, and spices.

Roger's Chocolate Fruit & Nut Muffins. Cocoa powder, chocolate syrup, raisins, roasted walnuts, sour cream, and a hint of orange peel.

Rum Raisin Muffins. Golden raisins, applesauce, vanilla yogurt, rum flavoring, and spice.

Sugar Plum Fairy Muffins. Orange and lemon peel, applesauce, sour cream, and plum glaze topping with a sprinkling of pearl sugar.

White Chocolate with Raspberries Muffins. White chocolate, fresh raspberries, and sour cream.

6. Extra-Effort-But-Worth-It Muffins

These muffins take more than the usual 10 or 15 minutes to prepare, but I think you'll agree they're worth it.

Blueberry-Peach Schnapps Muffins. Fresh blueberries and peach purée, with a peach schnapps glaze.

Cinnamon Sticky Muffins. Roasted walnuts, sunflower seeds, applesauce, and cinnamon.

Charity Nut Muffins. Roasted walnuts, toasted wheat germ, and buttermilk.

Devil's Food Muffins with Vanilla Cream Cheese Icing. Chocolate syrup, cocoa powder, mini semi-sweet chocolate chips, and cream cheese icing.

Flipped Apple Muffins. Apples, applesauce, oat bran, and a hint of rum flavoring and lemon peel.

Gingerbread Muffins with Lemon Curd Filling. Fresh ginger root, molasses, orange peel, buttermilk, spices, and a lemon curd filling.

Glazed Ginger-Carrot Muffins. Carrots, fresh ginger root, and orange peel.

Glazed Sunrise Blueberry Muffins. Blueberries, lemon peel, and orange peel.

Grand Marnier Creamsicle Muffins. Orange peel, vanilla, sour cream, and a Grand Marnier glaze.

Jim Dandy Jelly Crumb Muffins. All-fruit jelly, buttermilk, and a cinnamon crumble topping.

Marvelous Marble Muffins with Coffee Icing. Semi-sweet chocolate chips, cocoa powder, buttermilk, and coffee-flavored cream cheese icing.

Pineapple Upside-Down Muffins. Crushed pineapple, applesauce, lemon peel, margarine or butter, and buttermilk.

Wantana's Thai Custard Muffins. Flaked coconut, sour cream, coconut milk, and vanilla custard sauce.

Wheat Berry Surprise Muffins. Wheat berries, assorted flours, molasses, and lemon peel.

Wheat Berry and Date Muffins. Wheat berries, rolled oats, dates, and a brown sugar-cinnamon topping.

7. Low-Fat-and-Still-Yummy Muffins

Every muffin in this chapter is low-fat—that is, they contain 3 grams of fat or less!

Almond-Cardamom-Fig Muffins. Dried figs, sliced almonds, applesauce, and cardamom.

Apple-Ginger Muffins. Fresh apples, applesauce, and crystallized ginger.

Berry Berry Delicious Muffins. Dried raspberries, dried cranberries, apple juice concentrate, and nonfat sour cream.

Black Cherry Blossom Muffins. Dark sweet cherries, applesauce, and a light touch of lemon peel.

Blueberries, Oats, and Cream Muffins. Fresh blueberries, rolled oats, oat bran, nonfat sour cream, and lemon peel.

Café Crumble Muffins. Triple-strength coffee, nonfat yogurt, honey, and a crumble topping.

Chocolate-Covered Cherry Muffins. Dark sweet cherries, mini semi-sweet chocolate chips, cocoa powder, nonfat sour cream, and cherry flavoring.

Chocolate Chip-Banana Muffins. Ripe bananas and mini semi-sweet chocolate chips.

Coco Nana Muffins. Flaked coconut, ripe bananas, and orange peel.

Cottage Cheese and Pear Muffins. Nonfat cottage cheese, fresh or canned pears, honey, and a hint of cardamom.

Cranberry-Apple Muffins. Dried cranberries, fresh apples, apple juice concentrate, nonfat buttermilk, spice, and a hint of rum flavoring.

Double Ginger Ginger Muffins. Crystallized ginger, golden raisins, a hint of molasses, and lots of spice.

Hillsborough House Inn Breakfast Muffins. Currants, sweet potato purée, dark brown sugar, molasses, and spices, with a roasted walnut and honey crunch wheat germ topping.

Orange-Strawberry-Banana Muffins. Ripe bananas, orange peel, and strawberry flavoring

Pineapple-Carrot-Ginger Muffins. Carrots, dried pineapple, fresh ginger root, and vanilla cream cheese icing.

Ricotta Cheese with Basil and Rosemary Muffins. Rye flour, low-fat ricotta cheese, vegetable broth, fresh basil, and fresh rosemary.

Scarborough Fair Muffins. Rye flour, nonfat buttermilk, vegetable broth, fresh sage, rosemary, thyme, and a hint of honey.

Toasted Wheat Germ Crunch Muffins. Nonfat buttermilk, apple juice concentrate, maple syrup, and toasted wheat germ-brown sugar topping.

Index

MRS. CUBBISON'S BEST STUFFING COOKBOOK
Sensational Stuffings for Poultry, Meats, Fish, Side Dishes, and More
Edited by Leo Pearlstein and Lisa Messinger

When you think of stuffing, you probably picture Thanksgiving, turkey, and traditional dinner fare. But now that people all over the country are enjoying exciting new flavors, from fusion cooking to ethnic cuisine, maybe it's time to add a little pizzazz to your stuffing—and to your everyday meals, as well! Designed to take stuffing to new culinary heights, here is a superb collection of creative recipes from America's number-one stuffing expert, Mrs. Sophie Cubbison.

Mrs. Cubbison's Best Stuffing Cookbook is a complete guide to the art of making delicious stuffing. It begins with the basics of preparing stuffing, and then offers 100 easy-to-make kitchen tested recipes—from Jambalaya Stuffing to Asian Ginger Stir-Fried, and from Citrus Yam Stuffing to Onion Soufflé. Within its "Shaping Up" chapter, you'll learn how to turn stuffing into mouth-watering muffins, pick-up appetizers, and tempting desserts. Mrs. Cubbison has even included delicious low-fat, reduced-calorie recipes!

For over sixty years, pioneering chef Mrs. Cubbison reinvented the way we cook with stuffing. Today, her company lives on to reflect our ever-evolving tastes. With *Mrs. Cubbison's Best Stuffing Cookbook* in hand, you can add a touch of creativity not only to your holiday celebrations, but to every meal that you and your family enjoy.

$14.95 US / $22.50 CAN • 156 Pages • 7.5 x 7.5-inch quality paperback • Cooking/Stuffings • ISBN 0-7570-0260-9

THE SOURDOUGH BREAD BOWL COOKBOOK
For Parties, Holiday Celebrations, Family Gatherings, and Everyday Meals
John Vrattos and Lisa Messinger

For decades, visitors to San Francisco's famed Fisherman's Wharf have enjoyed piping hot clam chowder served in a crusty sourdough bread bowl. As the popularity of this culinary treat grew, so did the many creative uses of bread bowls—from centerpieces filled with luscious dips to edible vessels for salads, entrées, and more. Gourmet cook John Vrattos and best-selling food writer Lisa Messinger have created a cookbook to show you how. After presenting easy-to-follow instructions for carving out a bread bowl, they offer over 100 sumptuous kitchen-tested recipes, ranging from traditional dishes such as Fisherman's Wharf-Style Clam Chowder to innovative creations like Teriyaki Chicken Bowl and Popcorn Shrimp Gumbo. Throughout the book, you'll also find outstanding bread bowl recipes developed by a number of top restaurant chefs.

Whether you're hosting a Super Bowl party, preparing a meal for the family, or simply cooking an intimate dinner for two, make your event a little more special with a selection from *The Sourdough Bread Bowl Cookbook*.

$14.95 US / $22.50 CAN • 144 Pages • 7.5 x 7.5-inch quality paperback • Cooking / Bread Bowls • ISBN 0-7570-0149-1

THE MASON JAR COOKIE COOKBOOK
How to Create Mason Jar Cookie Mixes
Lonnette Parks

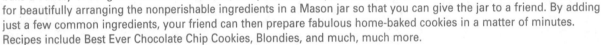

Nothing gladdens the heart like the tantalizing aroma of cookies baking in the oven. But for so many people, a busy lifestyle has made it impossible to find the time to bake at home—until now. Lonnette Parks, cookie baker extraordinaire, has not only developed fifty kitchen-tested recipes for delicious cookies, but has found a way for you to give the gift of home baking to everyone on your gift list.

For each mouth-watering cookie, the author provides the full recipe so that you can bake a variety of delights at home. In addition, she presents complete instructions for beautifully arranging the nonperishable ingredients in a Mason jar so that you can give the jar to a friend. By adding just a few common ingredients, your friend can then prepare fabulous home-baked cookies in a matter of minutes. Recipes include Best Ever Chocolate Chip Cookies, Blondies, and much, much more.

Whether you want to bake scrumptious cookies in your own kitchen or you'd like to give distinctive Mason jar cookie mixes to cookie-loving friends and family, *The Mason Jar Cookie Cookbook* is the perfect book.

$12.95 US / $21.00 CAN • 144 pages • 7.5 x 7.5-inch quality paperback • 2-Color • Cooking/Baking/Cookies • ISBN 0-7570-0046-0

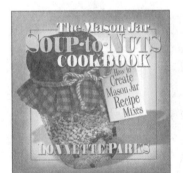

THE MASON JAR SOUP-TO-NUTS COOKBOOK
How to Create Mason Jar Recipe Mixes
Lonnette Parks

In this follow-up to her best-selling book, *The Mason Jar Cookie Cookbook,* author and cook Lonnette Parks presents recipes for over fifty delicious soups, muffins, breads, cakes, pancakes, beverages, and more. And, just as in her previous book, the author tells you how to give the gift of home cooking to friends and family.

For each Mason jar creation, the author provides the full recipe so that you can cook and bake a variety of delights at home. In addition, she includes complete instructions for beautifully arranging the nonperishable ingredients in a Mason jar so that you can give the jar to a friend. Recipes include Golden Corn Bread, Double Chocolate Biscotti, Ginger Muffins, Apple Cinnamon Pancakes, Barley Rice Soup, Viennese Coffee, and much, much more.

$12.95 US / $21.00 CAN • 144 pages • 7.5 x 7.5-inch quality paperback • 2-Color • Cooking/ Crafts • ISBN 0-7570-0129-7